HAYDN'S
VISITS TO
ENGLAND

JOSEPH HAYDN BY HOPPNER

Christopher Hogwood

HAYDN'S VISITS TO ENGLAND

Thames & Hudson

The publisher would like to thank H. C. Robbins Landon
and Barrie & Jenkins for permission to quote from *The Collected
Correspondence and London Notebooks of Joseph Haydn*, and
Haydn: Chronicle and Works. Haydn in England 1791–5.

First published in the United Kingdom in 1980 by The Folio Society Limited

Reprinted with corrections in 2009 by Thames & Hudson Ltd,
181A High Holborn, London WC1V 7QX

www.thamesandhudson.com

British Library Cataloguing-in-Publication Data
A catalogue record for this book is available from the British Library

ISBN 978-0-500-51460-3

Printed and bound in China by Everbest Co. Ltd.

To my father

CONTENTS

ILLUSTRATIONS

PRELUDE

Haydn's life story, he himself insisted, could interest nobody. For his own epitaph he suggested simply *Vixi, scripsi, dixi*: I lived, I wrote, I spoke. His life was marked by no great event; he had accepted the conditions of eighteenth-century court patronage, working as Kapellmeister to Prince Nicolaus Esterházy under a contract as prohibitive as any domestic servant would have been expected to sign, and he posed for his portrait wearing court livery like a footman. He worked conscientiously and regularly, attending to the needs of an orchestra, an opera company and a music-loving patron. The miraculous flowering of his rare talent which took place during nearly thirty years he spent in the Esterházys' remote rococo palace was curtly described: 'I was cut off from the world, and I was forced to become original.'

Fortunately two non-musicians were persistent enough to draw from Haydn in his old age in Vienna an account of some of the incidents of his life. Both Georg Griesinger, a diplomat attached to the Saxon Legation, and Albert Christoph Dies, a mediocre painter, published biographical accounts of Haydn's life in 1810, on which all later writers lean heavily. They each reported many incidents as *verbatim* accounts from the composer himself, and Griesinger made use of a number of notebooks that Haydn had kept during the 1790s (including one which has since disappeared). Haydn's own writings also include a large number of letters, many to his prince and his publishers, but some, more personal, to his mistress Luigia Polzelli, and to the wife of one of Prince Nicolaus's doctors, Maria Anna von Genzinger. The newspaper clippings that Haydn himself collected indicate a further source of contemporary material, and to these we can add a plenitude of diaries, memoirs, recollections and reminiscences, not only from historians such as Charles Burney, but painters like Farington, retired musicians such as Parke, and gossipy society ladies in the manner of Mrs Papendiek.

To achieve some perspective on the material, one must turn to the work of H. C. Robbins Landon, the doyen of modern Haydn scholarship, without whose efforts much of the prime source material might never have come to light. His five-volume survey, *Haydn: Chronicle and Works*, a monument of perspicacity and enthusiasm, is both model and quarry for later researchers. His translations of Haydn's own writings are used in this volume, and full references to these and all other quoted material are given at the end of the book and indicated at the end of each quotation. English sources are reproduced in their original spelling and punctuation.

At a distance of some two hundred years it is disconcerting to realize how, while Haydn's music had travelled the world over, the man himself had hardly been seen outside Vienna and Esterháza. Even allowing for his innate modesty, his affection for his prince would surely have stirred him to deny the exaggerated accounts of his predicament that travellers began to retail. Gaetano Bartolozzi, for example, the son of the famous artist, went to visit him and reported that his pay was less than the most obscure fiddler in London would accept, his miserable apartment in the barracks furnished with no more than a bed and an old spinet.

Haydn himself, though, took a more stoical view of his situation. Early in 1785 the London papers took up the story . . .

HAYDN'S FIRST VISIT

'There is something very distressing to a liberal mind in the history of *Haydn*. This wonderful man, who is the Shakespeare of music, and the triumph of the age in which we live, is doomed to reside in the court of a miserable German Prince, who is at once incapable of rewarding him, and unworthy of the honour. *Haydn*, the simplest as well as the greatest of men, is resigned to his condition, and in devoting his life to the rites and ceremonies of the Roman Catholic Church, which he carries even to superstition, is content to live immured in a place little better than a dungeon, subject to the domineering spirit of a petty Lord, and the clamourous temper of a scolding wife. Would it not be an achievement equal to a pilgrimage, for some aspiring youths to rescue him from his fortune and transplant him to Great Britain, the country for which his music seems to be made?' (17.i.85)

Despite such encouragement from the *Gazetteer & New Daily Advertiser*, the British public of 1785 did not rally to the call of kidnapping Haydn for the benefit of England and his own soul. They had been tantalized for upwards of two years by the prospect of a visit from Europe's greatest composer, but their hopes had been unremittingly dashed.

The Earl of Abingdon, who had taken over the running of the Bach–Abel concert series, confidently announced the engagement of Haydn for his 1782 season in London's newest purpose-built concert hall, the Hanover Square Rooms (traditionally, but inaccurately, always referred to in the plural).

'The Shakespeare of musical composition is hourly expected' declared the *Morning Herald* for 23 November 1782. Two days later the same paper was less confident:

'The *musical world* are rather alarmed, lest the celebrated *Haydn* should decline visiting England. His stay is so much

A Bravura at the Hanover Square Concert.

London: Pub.d by Will.m Holland, N.o 50 Oxford Street May 27, 178.

In Holland's Exhibition Rooms may be seen the largest Collection of humorous Prints in our

courted by persons of the first fashion and eminence on the continent, so engaged is he in his studious avocations and domestic concerns, that Lord Abingdon has yet received no positive assurance that he will come over.'

Hopes rose again on the 27th ('Hayden certainly joins his Talents to the Band') but were unfulfilled even by the following February, whereat 'we understand that the noble conductors of this fashionable assembly are not a little *disconcerted* themselves!' The perseverance of the press is, in itself, some indication of the public demand for Haydn in person. By July, his native prudence was adduced as apology for his tardiness.

'The great Hayden, next autumn, comes to London. Phlegm, and, in all pecuniary concerns, extreme caution, are among the leading characteristics of this great composer; insomuch so, that last winter he could not, without uncommon assurances, be prevailed upon to send his new music over to Lord Abingdon's Grand Concert.'

(*Morning Post* 19.vii.83)

Lord Abingdon, that great man of the turf, appeared to be backing a loser.

But the would-be crusaders were unjustified; Haydn was not imprisoned either by his prince or even his church; he was loyal to both and the spell was only broken by the death of Nicolaus Esterházy on 28 September 1790. Two days later his successor Prince Anton sacked the entire orchestra and opera company! All that he retained was a small wind-band, the most economic and utilitarian grouping for ceremonial purposes. The remainder of the enormous establishment made their escape from the chilly marshes of Hungary. Haydn returned to Vienna and a rented apartment. There, on what amounted to a retirement pension from Prince Anton, he turned down an offer of employment from Prince Grassalkovics, and toyed for a few weeks with the idea of a position with the King of Naples. But one evening an unannounced visitor arrived:

'I am Salomon of London and have come to fetch you. Tomorrow we will arrange an *accord*.'

Salomon's bravura paid off. He had been amongst the many enthusiasts in England who had petitioned Haydn for years to come to London. He himself, a German-born violinist and a generous and efficient impresario, now had his own concert series in London, and an acceptance from Haydn would be the *coup* of the season. Charming, business-like, and with the London public behind him, he could make the scheme financially attractive. An '*accord*' was soon reached on terms that far exceeded anything Haydn had been used to receiving from the Esterházys: £300 for an opera (this on behalf of 'Sir John' Gallini* and the King's Theatre), £300 for six symphonies for Salomon's series, plus £200 for the copyright on these, £200 for twenty other new compositions, and a guaranteed minimum of £200 from a Benefit Concert for himself. No mention of actual performance: Haydn was, on his own confession, 'no Wizard' as either violinist or pianist.

Mozart, who was, came to a small farewell dinner-party with Salomon and his friend Haydn; he, of course, had seen London as a child some twenty-five years before, and tried to dissuade Haydn from the venture: 'You won't stand it for long, you'll soon return; you aren't young any more.' 'But I'm still vigorous and in good health,' answered Haydn. 'You have had no education for the great world, and you speak too few languages.' 'Oh!' replied Haydn, 'my language is understood all over the world.'

On the day of his departure, 15 December 1790, Mozart never left Haydn. They dined together, and at the moment of parting Mozart said, 'We are probably saying our last adieu in this life.' Haydn, at fifty-eight, took the remark to apply to himself – as it turned out he was wrong, though his friend's premonitions were correct: Mozart died a year later, at the age of thirty-five, while Haydn was still in London.

* The title was informal, based on the Papal award of the Knighthood of the Golden Spur (a decoration also given to Gluck and Mozart). Giovanni Gallini was a successful dancing-master.

By New Year's Eve the travellers had reached Calais. On New Year's Day Haydn embarked on his first sea voyage, and on 2 January 1791 arrived at last in London. A few days later he wrote to his friend Maria Anna von Genzinger, the wife of the Esterházys' physician:

'*London 8 January 1791*

'Nobly born,
Gracious Lady!
I hope that you will have received my last letter from Calais. I should have written you immediately after my arrival in London, but I wanted to wait a few days so as to be able to write about several things at once. So I can tell you that on the 1st inst., New Year's Day, after attending early mass, I boarded the ship at 7:30 a.m. and at 5 in the afternoon I arrived, thank God! safe and sound in Dower. At the beginning, for the first 4 whole hours, we had almost no wind, and the ship went so slowly that in these 4 hours we didn't go further than one single English mile, and there are 24 between Calais and Dower. Our ship's captain, in an evil temper, said that if the wind did not change, we should have to spend the whole night at sea. Fortunately, however, towards 11:30 o'clock a wind arose and blew so favourably that by 4 o'clock we covered 22 miles. Since the tide, which had just begun to ebb, prevented our large vessel from reaching the pier, 2 smaller ships came out to meet us as we were still fairly far out at sea, and into these we and our luggage were transferred, and thus at last, though exposed to a medium gale, we landed safely. The large vessel stood out to sea five hours longer, till the tide turned and it could finally dock. Some of the passengers were afraid to board the little boats and stayed on board, but I followed the example of the greater number. I remained on deck during the whole passage, so as to gaze my fill at that mighty monster, the ocean. So long as it was calm, I wasn't afraid at all, but towards the end, when the wind grew stronger and stronger, and I saw the monstrous high waves rushing at us, I became a little frightened, and a little indisposed, too. But I overcame it all and arrived safely, without (excuse me) vomiting,

on shore. Most of the passengers were ill, and looked like ghosts, but since I went on to London, I didn't feel the effects of the journey right away; but then I needed 2 days to recover. Now, however, I am fresh and well again, and occupied in looking at this endlessly huge city of London, whose various beauties and marvels quite astonished me. I immediately paid the necessary calls, such as to the Neapolitan Ambassador and to our own; both called on me in return 2 days later, and 4 days ago I lunched with the former – N.B. at 6 o'clock in the evening, as is the custom here.

'My arrival caused a great sensation throughout the whole city, and I went the round of all the newspapers for 3 successive days. Everyone wants to know me. I had to dine out 6 times up to now, and if I wanted, I could dine out every day; but first I must consider my health, and 2nd my work. Except for the nobility, I admit no callers till 2 o'clock in the afternoon, and at 4 o'clock I dine at home with *Mon.* Salomon. I have nice and comfortable, but expensive, lodgings. My landlord is Italian, and also a cook, and serves me 4 very respectable meals; we each pay 1 fl. 30 kr. a day excluding wine and beer, but everything is terribly expensive here. Yesterday I was invited to a grand amateur concert, but I arrived a bit late, and when I showed my ticket they wouldn't let me in but led me to an antichamber, where I had to wait till the piece which was then being played in the hall was over. Then they opened the door, and I was conducted, on the arm of the *entrepreneur*, up the centre of the hall to the front of the orchestra, amid universal applause, and there I was stared at and greeted by a great number of English compliments. I was assured that such honours had not been conferred on anyone for 50 years. After the concert I was taken to a handsome adjoining room, where a table for 200 persons, with many places set, was prepared for all the amateurs; I was supposed to be seated at the head of the table, but since I had dined out on that day and had eaten more than usual, I declined this honour, with the excuse that I was not feeling very well, but despite this I had to drink the harmonious health, in Burgundy, of all the gentlemen present; they all returned the toast, and then allowed me to be taken home. All this, my gracious lady, was very flattering to me, and yet I wished I could fly for a time to Vienna, to have more quiet in which to work, for the noise that the common people make as they sell their wares in the street is intolerable. At present I am working on symphonies, because the libretto of the opera is not yet decided on, but in order to have more quiet I shall have to rent a room far from the centre of town. I would gladly write you in more detail, but I am afraid of missing the mail-coach. Meanwhile I am, with kindest regards to your husband, *Fräulein* Pepi and all the others, most respectfully.

Your Grace's

most sincere and obedient servant,

Joseph Haydn'   (CCLN III–13)

Salomon had obviously done his public relations work well, almost too well. Luckily Haydn's shrewdness and resilience got him through those first exhausting days, and his new-found freedom did not turn his head. Here, for the first time, he was liberated from the coolness and restraint implicit in the system of court patronage in Europe; here both public and orchestra rose to their feet to welcome him, kings and princes nodded even without introduction!

'A remarkable Circumstance happened on Thursday Evening. In the Ball-Room at St James's: Haydn, the celebrated Composer, though he has not yet been introduced at our Court, was recognized by all the Royal Family, and paid them his silent Respects. Mr Haydn came into the Room with Sir John Gallini, Mr Wills and Mr Salomon. The Prince of Wales first observed him, and upon bowing to him, the Eyes of all the Company were upon Mr Haydn, every one paying him Respect.'   (*Daily Advertiser* 20.i. 91)

Dr Charles Burney, famed for his *General History of Music* (and his daughter Fanny), was one of Haydn's staunchest hero-worshippers, and showed his respect in more tangible form. He had been angling for this visit since 1783 ('but mum mum mum – yet – a correspondence is opened, & there is a great likelihood of it, if these Cabals, & litigations ruin not the Opera completely'). Now he hurried to present Haydn with the four volumes of his *History* 'superbly bound' together with a set of verses 'on the arrival in England of the great musician Haydn'. To make sure Haydn appreciated his poetic gifts, Burney had the verses put into German by his good friend the musician Ignatius Latrobe, to whom he wrote:

'Having met the $\left\{ \begin{array}{l} \text{good} \\ \text{great} \end{array} \right.$ man, by accident, at the Professional Concert soon after he had rec^d my present, he took the opportunity of making *fine speeches* innumerable, *viva voce*, & by that means saved himself the trouble of writing a letter, as he told me he intended to do. I afterwards met him at the Concert of Anc^t Music in Tottenham street, whence I carried him home when it was over; & then he repeated & added more *fine things* on my present, than he c^d have written on ten sheets of Paper.'   (Lonsdale 353)

Mistaking Haydn's tact for approval, however, Burney expanded the poem and had it published anonymously. 'I must entreat you to keep my secret,' he warned Latrobe, 'or I shall have all the envious brethren on my back' – a modesty which, we note, allowed Burney to welcome both poem and composer in the *Monthly Review*. The poem received a cooler reception from Burney's friend the Rev. Twining, who pronounced it 'dry, prosaic, and cataloguish', a view which cannot be contradicted even by a careful selection of stanzas.

VERSES on the ARRIVAL of *HAYDN* in england

> *Music! The Calm of life, the cordial bowl,*
> *Which anxious care can banish from the soul,*
> *Affliction soothe, and elevate the mind,*
> *And all its sordid manacles unbind,*
> *Can snatch us from life's incidental pains,*
> *And 'wrap us in Elysium with its strains!'*
> *To cultivated ears, this fav'rite art*
> *No new delights was able to impart;*
> *No Eagle flights its votaries durst essay,*
> *But hopp'd, like little birds, from spray to spray.*

*

Our Tallis, Bird *and matchless* Purcell, *still*
Each sacred dome with sounds seraphic fill;
But grace and elegance, to them unknown,
(Of which elsewhere, no seeds had yet been sown)
With strains impassion'd for the lyric scene,
From foreign fields we are ever forc'd to glean;
And long from these our Instruments were fed,
And Concerts furnish'd with their daily bread;
Till dry and stale became, they ceas'd, at last,
To please and charm us in the ear's repast.

At length great HAYDN'S *new and varied strains*
Of habit and indiff'rence broke the chains;
Rous'd to attention the long torpid sense,
With all that pleasing wonder could dispense.

Artists who long their trade had exercis'd,
No less than feeling ignorance, were surpriz'd
At strains so new, to hand, to eye, and ear,
As made them Tiros *in their art appear.*
Whene'er Parnassus' height he meant to climb,
Whether the grand, pathetic, or sublime,
The simply graceful, or the comic vein,
The theme suggested, or enrich'd the strain,
From melting sorrow to gay jubilation,
Whate'er his pen produc'd was Inspiration!

*

Haydn! Great Sovereign of the tuneful art!
Thy works alone supply an ample chart
Of all the mountains, seas, and fertile plains,
Within the compass of its wide domains.
Is there an Artist of the present day
Untaught by thee to think, as well as play?
Whose hand thy science has not well supplied?
Whose hand thy labours have not fortified?

*

Welcome, great Master! to our favour'd Isle,
Already partial to thy name and style;
Long may thy fountain of invention run
In streams as rapid as first begun;
While skill for each fantastic whim provides,
And certain science ev'ry current guides!
Oh, may thy days, from human suff'rings free,
Be blest with glory and felicity!
With full fruition, to a distant hour,
Of all thy magic and creative pow'r!
Blest in thyself, with rectitude of mind;
And blessing, with thy talents, all mankind!

Burney's other efforts on Haydn's behalf were more successful than his poetry; on 24 April 1791 he wrote enthusiastically to the Rev. Twining of private music parties that he
organized in Chelsea College, where he now had rooms:

'I ⟨spent⟩ the day yesterday with the dear great & good
Haydn, whom I love more & more every time I see as well as
hear him. In a small party chiefly of my own family, we
prevailed on him to play the 1ˢᵗ Violin to his Instrumental
Passione, for wᶜʰ, though we cᵈ only perform it in 4 parts,
though it consists of 16, yet its effect was admirable as
executed by him, in a most chaste & feeling manner. He
played the 2ᵈ Violin only to several of his Quartets – while
my Nephews played the 1ˢᵗ & Tenor, & a Mʳ Gun of Cambridge the Violoncello.'   (Lonsdale 354)

The *Instrumental Passione* was an arrangement for string quartet of *The Seven Last Words of Christ*, which Burney described
as 'perhaps, the most sublime composition without words to
point out its meaning that has ever been composed'. The
same work, this time with Haydn playing the 'Tenor' (i.e.
the viola), was laid on again in May to satisfy the excited
Rev. Twining, up in town from Colchester:

'I don't know anything – any musical thing – that would
delight me so much as to meet him in a snug quartet party,
and hear his manner of playing his own music. If you can

bring about such a thing while I am in town, either at
Chelsea, or at Mr Burney's [i.e. Charles's son], or at Mr
Salomon's, or at I care not where, if it were even in the black
hole at Calcutta (if it is a good hole for music) – I say, if by
hook or by crook you could manage such a thing, you should
be my Magnus Apollo for the rest of your life.'

(Twining 147)

One wonders in which language these musical meetings
were conducted. Burney, we know, was far from competent
in German, while Haydn's command of English was, to say
the least, rudimentary. However, despite Mozart's fears,
Haydn's ingenuity seems to have found ways round the
problem. The Rev. Christian Ignatius Latrobe, who was not
only the translator of Burney's verses and an amateur musician and composer, but also a minister in the Moravian
church, reports on Haydn's first visit to his home:

'I was introduced to him by Dr Burney, who well knew the
value I should set upon the personal acquaintance of a man,

whose Works I so greatly admired, and of which I may say, that they had been a feast to my soul . . . he was pleased, not long after, to pay me a visit. When he entered the room, he found my wife alone, & as she could not speak German, & he had scarcely picked up a few English words, both were at a loss what to say. He bowed with foreign formality, & the following short Explanation took place.

H: "Dis, Mr Latrobe house?" The answer was in the affirmative.

H: "Be you his Woman?" (meaning his wife).

"I am Mrs Latrobe," was the reply.

After some pause, he looked round the room, & saw his picture, to which he immediately pointed, & exclaimed, "Dat is me. I am Haydn!" My wife instantly, knowing what a most welcome guest I was honoured with, sent for me to a house not far off, & treated him with all possible civility. He was meanwhile amused with some fine specimens of Labrador spar on the Chimney-piece, which he greatly admired & accepted of a polished slab. Of course I hastened home, & passed half an hour with him in agreeable conversation.'

(Landon 57)

The friendship flourished, and Latrobe took to calling on Haydn at his lodgings, where he was treated to extracts from works in progress.

'On enquiry, hearing from a friend, that I had ventured to compose some Sonatas for the Pianoforte, he desired to hear them. As he observed, that they ought to be printed, I agreed, if he would permit me to dedicate them to him. Of this he has made mention in his own account of his Visits to England.'

(Landon 58)

The 'account of his Visits', which Latrobe mentions, is in fact nothing more formal than a series of jottings which Haydn made in four small notebooks while he was in London, and which were later quoted in part by his first biographers, Griesinger and Dies. Sure enough, in a list of the principal musicians in London (the names rendered with the most curious orthography), we find

> la Trobe—dedicated
> his piano Sonatas to
> me

(CCLN 263)

But these London Notebooks contain much more than simple lists; Haydn took to jotting down oddments of information, addresses, recipes, 'anectods' (as he called them), and almost any fact or phrase that caught his fancy, producing a wonderfully vivid document of his endless curiosity and humour. Most of the notes are in German, but a few tax the imagination with his own idiosyncratic English. His first English shopping list, for instance, reads:

Head of June, white Cornelian	6	guinees
that other white red Cornelian	$3\frac{1}{2}$	guinees
6 Schirts	8	—
12 deto	12	—
watch from gold	30	—
the chen	1	—

(CCLN 251)

A head of Juno, 6 shirts, 12 ditto and a gold watch and chain can just about be construed. Prices and numbers in general fascinated him and also any facts about the sea and ships (understandably, since the Channel crossing had been the first sea-voyage of his life). Food and drink share the pages with musical scandal and moral reflections. Sadly, some of the more *immoral* anecdotes are tantalizingly unfinished:

'The little story of an errand boy who ate cow dung . . .'

'Duchess of Devonchire . . . Anecdote about the foot under her petticoat . . .'

'Mr Fox's trousers. Story of a sedan-chair-bearer. He lost £4000 but got them back by this clever idea . . .'

Others, though, are devastatingly complete:
'In France the girls are virtuous and the wives are whores; in Holland the girls are whores and the wives are virtuous: in England they stay whores all their lives.'

The majority of entries reveal Haydn's insatiable curiosity (and occasional astonishment) at English manners, morals and customs.

'If anybody steals £2 he is hanged; but if I trust anybody with £2000, and he carries it off to the devil, he is acquitted. Murder and forgery cannot be pardoned; last year a clergyman was hanged for the latter, even though the King himself did all he could for him.'

'The City of London consumes 8 times one hundred thousand cartloads of coal each year; each cart holds 13 sacks, each sack holds 2 dry measures [= 3.44 litre]: most of the coal comes from Newcastle. Often 200 loaded ships arrive at once. A cartload costs £2½.'

'If a woman murders her husband, she is burned alive, whereas the husband, on the contrary, is hanged.'

'The punishment of a murderer is increased, when sentence is passed on him, by the fact that his body is dissected after his death.'

'During the last 31 years, 38,000 houses were built in London.'

'The City of London keeps 4,000 carts for cleaning the streets, and 2,000 of these work every day.'

'The national debt of England is estimated to be over two hundred millions. Recently it was calculated that if they had to make up a convoy to pay this sum in silver, the waggons, end on end, would reach from London to Yorck, that is, 200 miles, presuming that each waggon could not carry more than £6000.'

'In Oxford Street I saw St Peter engraved in copper; he was clad as a secular priest with outstretched arms. The glory of heaven shines on his right side, and on his left you see the devil, whispering in his ear, and with a wind-mill on his head.'

'Lord Clermont [Claremont] once gave a large *Soupé*, and when the King's health was drunk, he ordered the wind band to play the well-known song, "God save the King" in the street during a wild snowstorm. This occurred on 19 Feby 1792, so madly do they drink in England.'

'At the beginning of May 1792, Lord Barrymore gave a ball that cost 5,000 guineas. He paid 1,000 guineas for 1,000 peaches. 2000 baskets of gusberes [gooseberries], 5 shillings a basket.'

'In the month of January 1792, a roasting chicken cost 7 shillings, a turkey 9 shillings, a dozen larks 1 crown. N.B.: a duck, if it is plucked, costs 5 shillings.'

'Noyan, a drink. Squeezed from nutmeg, rum and sugar. Comes from Martinique in the West Indies, which belongs to France.'

'Oranges from Portugal arrive in the middle of November, but they are quite pale and not so good as they are later.'

'In order to preserve cream or milk for a long time, one takes a bottle full of milk and puts it in an earthenware pot or copper vessel containing water enough to cover more than half of the bottle, and then places it over a fire and lets it simmer half-an-hour. Then one takes the bottle out and seals it securely, so that no air can escape, and in this way the milk will keep for many months. N.B.: The bottle must be securely corked before it is placed in the water.
     This was told me by a sea captain.'

'In the month of August [1791] I lunched at noon on an East India merchantman with 6 cannon. I was given a magnificent meal.'

'In England, a large man-of-war is reckoned according to the number of its cannon. Each cannon is estimated at 1,000 lbs.'

'When a Quaker goes to Court, he pays the door-keeper to take off his hat for him, for a Quaker takes his hat off to no one. In order to pay the King's tax, an official goes to his house during the period when the tax is being collected, and in his presence robs him of as much goods as represent the tax in value. When the disguised thief leaves the door with his goods, the Quaker calls him back and asks him how much money he wants for the stolen things. The official demands just the amount of the tax, and in this way the Quaker pays the tax to the King.'

'In solitude, too, there are divinely beautiful duties, and to perform them in quiet is more than wealth.'

(CCLN 253–78)

Sometime during the spring of 1791, only a few months after his arrival in London, Haydn decided to find his own solitude away from the social whirl (and street-cries) of central London, and moved to the countryside of Lisson Grove. There, where the Westbourne was still an open stream, flowing past cows grazing in green meadows, he settled down to work on his opera (the text selected was a version of Orpheus and Eurydice called *L'Anima del Filosofo*) and the symphonies promised to Salomon.

That impresario, meanwhile, was placating the public with daily apologies for the fact that his series had not yet opened; problems with the singers, he explained, prevented them appearing in his performances before they had been heard at the Opera, and 'rather than disappoint his subscribers by the Non-appearance of . . . etc.' By 11 March, however, all was ready:

HANOVER-SQUARE. MR SALOMON respectfully acquaints the Nobility and Gentry, that his CONCERTS will open without further delay on Friday next, the 11th of March, and continue every succeeding Friday.

PART I

Overture – Rosetti
Song – Sig Tajana
Concerto Oboe – Mr Harrington
Song – Signora Storace
Concerto Violin – Madame Gautherot
Recitativo and Aria – Signor David

GIACOMO DAVIDE

PART II
New Grand Overture – Haydn
Recitative and Aria – Signora Storace
Concertante, Pedal Harp and Pianoforte – Madame
Krumpholtz and Mr Dusseck
Composed by Mr Dusseck
Rondo – Signor David
Full Piece – Kozeluck
Mr HAYDN will be at the Harpsichord
Leader of the Band, Mr SALOMON.
Tickets transferable, as usual, Ladies to Ladies and
Gentlemen to Gentlemen only.
The Ladies' tickets are Green, the Gentlemen's Black.
The Subscribers are intreated to give particular orders to
their Coachmen to set down and take up at the Side Door in
the Street, with the Horses' Heads towards the Square.
The Door in the Square is for Chairs only.
(*Public Advertiser* 7.iii.91)

A 'numerous and very elegant' audience attended this musi-cal feast – all Haydn's new English friends, including the Burneys, together with the Rev. Thomas Twining, who was wondering whether Haydn still retained his old powers, and wrote to Burney on 15 February 1791:

'If the resources of any human composer could be inexhaust-ible, I should suppose Haydn's would; but as, after all, he is but a mortal, I am afraid he must soon get to the bottom of his genius-box.'   (Lonsdale 355)

Totally unworried, however, was Charlotte Papendiek, wife of the Royal flute-master; her problem was what to wear:

'My dress now had to be considered, which had come down to the two muslins and the printed cambrics . . . the puce satin being at its last gasp. My blue satin cloak was quite new, and trimmed with a beautiful dark fur. I consulted Mrs Barlow, who said it was most elegant to wear as a wrap when cold, and on warmer evenings just to hang on more loosely, and she thought that till Easter it would be a dress suitable for any public occasion. A cap to suit I purchased of her for 35s., and Kead dressed my hair for 2s. 6d. as usual, charging the same price if he pinned on.

'The wished-for night at length arrived, and as I was anxious to be near the performers I went early. Mr Papen-diek followed from Queen's House, and I got an excellent seat on a sofa at the right-hand side. The orchestra was arranged on a new plan. The pianoforte was in the centre, at each extreme end the double basses, then on each side two violoncellos, then two tenors or violas and two violins, and in the hollow of the piano a desk on a high platform for Salomon with his ripieno. At the back, verging down to a point at each end, all these instruments were doubled, giving the requisite number for a full orchestra. Still further back, raised high up, were drums, and other side the trumpets, trombones, bas-soons, oboes, clarinets, flutes, &c., in numbers according to the requirements of the symphonies and other music to be played on the different evenings.

'The concert opened with a symphony of Haydn's that he

28

brought with him, but which was not known in England. It consisted of four movements, pleasing lively, and good . . .

'The second act invarably opened with a new symphony composed for the night.* Haydn of course conducted his own music, and generally that of other composers, in fact all through the evening.

'Hanover Square Rooms are calculated to hold 800 persons exclusive of the performers. By the beginning of the second act we concluded that all had arrived who intended to come, and though we knew that Salomon's subscription list was not full, we had hoped for additions during the evening. But no; and I regret to make this observation of my countrymen, that until they know what value they are likely to receive for their money they are slow in coming forward with it. An undertaking of this magnitude, bringing such a superior man from his own country as Haydn to compose for an orchestra filled with the highest professional skill and talent, should have met with every encouragement, first to show respect to the stranger and then to Salomon, who lived among us and had done so much for the musical world, in this case having taken such infinite trouble and incurred so much risk.

'Now the anxious moment arrived, and Salomon having called "attention" with his bow, the company rose to a person and stood through the whole of the first movement.

'The effect was imposingly magnificent. The instruments might all be said to have an obbligato part, so perfectly was the whole combination conceived and carried out . . . and Salomon was wound up to a pitch of enthusiasm beyond himself. The public were satisfied, and Haydn was very properly taken up.

'His great talent is too well known for me to comment upon it. His twelve grand symphonies were composed expressly for this series of concerts, and he stands unrivalled in this style of composition. . . . Indeed, his amiability, his unbounded talent in many ways, and his humility withal, his liberality, and his every virtue could but bring him friends.'

(Papendiek II 289–97)

*Probably No. 92.

MRS PAPENDIEK
AND HER SON
FREDERICK BY
THOMAS LAWRENCE

HANOVER SQUARE CONCERT ROOMS

Mrs Papendiek's *Journals* were written late in her life, after she had retired as 'Assistant Keeper of the Wardrobe and Reader to Her Majesty Queen Charlotte'. They suffer from haziness of recollection and were caustically criticized by Fanny Burney in her least attractive manner ('To read the book tires the intellect of no one, though it would exhaust the patience of many'). The description of the amphitheatre arrangement of the orchestra, however, is valuable, since this lay-out seems to have been new to London and was followed for most of the next century. It must also have presented a particularly elegant sight, raised in tiers culminating with trumpets and drums. Salomon's band seems to have made a point of dress, since Sir George Smart, once a member of Salomon's orchestra, remembers that the players used to rehearse wearing their greatcoats, in order to save their best dress for the performance. There was no conductor as such, but the direction was shared between the leader (Salomon) and the keyboard-player. The more conservative newspapers refer to Haydn at the harpsichord, but Dr Burney, more aware of changes in fashion, states:

'Haydn himself presided at the piano-forte; and the sight of that renowned composer so electrified the audience, as to excite an attention and a pleasure superior to any that had ever, to my knowledge, been caused by instrumental music in England.' (Arblay III 132)

The press also reported enthusiastically:

'The long delayed Concert, undertaken this year by Mr SALOMON, took place last night, and was attended by a numerous and very elegant audience. A musical treat, under the immediate direction of the great HAYDN, promised the connoisseurs an exquisite repast, and they were not disappointed . . . A new grand overture by HAYDN, was received with the highest applause, and universally deemed a composition as pleasing as scientific. The audience was so enraptured, that by unanimous desire, the second movement was encored, and the third was vehemently demanded a second time also, but the modesty of the Composer prevailed too strongly to admit a repetition . . .'

(*Diary: or, Woodfall's Register* 12.iii.1791)

Only one point of censure seems to have penetrated the screen of superlatives and encores, and that was levelled at Haydn himself for, of all things, beating time. The critic was William Jackson of Exeter:

'Instrumental Music has been of late carried to so great perfection in London, by the consummate skill of the Performers, that any attempt to beat the time would be justly considered as entirely needless. I am sorry to remark, that the attention of the Audience, at one Concert, has been interrupted by the vulgarity of this exploded Practice, which is unworthy the supreme excellence of the Band and highly disgusting to the Company . . .'   (Jackson 25–6)

'Alas!' rejoined Burney, 'poor Haydn can do nothing right either in the eyes or ears of his present critic. There is a censure levelled at him . . . for marking the measure to his own *new* compositions: but as even the old compositions had never been performed under his direction, in this country, till the last winter, it was surely allowable for him to indicate to the orchestra the exact time in which he intended the several movements to be played, without offending the leader or subalterns of the excellent band which he had to conduct.'   (*Monthly Review* x.91)

Opposition to the conductor lasted in England for many years; when Spohr drew his baton from his pocket and gave the signal to begin at a Philharmonic Concert in 1820 the directors protested at the innovation. And before Haydn's *faux pas*, W. T. Parke, the oboist, tells in his *Musical Memoirs* of the confounding of a similar attempt as early as 1784:

'When the time of performance had arrived, and Mr Cramer, the leader, had just tapt his bow, (the signal for being ready,) and looked round to catch the eyes of the performers, he saw, to his astonishment, a tall gigantic figure [Dr Philip Hayes, Professor of Music at Oxford], with an immense powdered toupée, fully dressed, with a bag and sword, and a huge roll of parchment in his hand.

' "Who is that gentleman?" said Mr Cramer. – "Dr Hayes," was the reply. – "What is he going to do?" – "To beat time." – "Be so kind," said Mr Cramer, "to tell the gentleman that when he has sat down I will begin." '

(Parke I 39)

Haydn was openly pleased with the practice of encoring individual movements – particularly slow movements, which was obviously something new for the English:

'At the first concert of Mr Salomon I created a furor with a new Symphony, and they had to repeat the Adagio: this had never before occurred in London. Imagine what it means to hear such a thing from an Englishman's lips.' (CCLN 116)

But he had also been quick to learn the importance of placing his own compositions in the second half of the programme, to avoid the less mannerly habits of English concert-going:

'The first act was usually disturbed in various ways by the noise of late-comers. Not a few persons came from well-set tables (where the men, as is the custom of the country, stay in the dining room and drink, after the ladies have left following the conclusion of the meal); they took a comfortable seat in the concert room and were so gripped by the magic of the music that they went fast to sleep.' (Dies: Landon 44)

Salomon's second concert was honoured with the presence of the Prince of Wales; but since the *Morning Chronicle* divulged that 'he came just in time to join in the triumph of Haydn', we can deduce that he missed at least the first half of the concert.

Salomon's series went from strength to strength, while the morning papers strained to exceed the adulation of the previous week. The Bohemian pianist Dussek appeared in the third concert playing his own concerto, and was, we are told, the first to place his instrument sideways upon the platform. In addition to concertos and a symphony (still termed 'overture' in England), each concert would have a number of vocal items (mostly featuring the tenor Davide, and the young Miss Corri*) and often an unpublished string quartet played by Salomon's quartet.

At the Opera House in the Haymarket, however, things were not running as smoothly as they were at Hanover Square. The old King's Theatre, the original theatre on that site, had burnt – or been burnt – down two years earlier ('Nothing but a conflagration ever produces uniform scenery') and 'Sir John' Gallini, in rebuilding the establishment, had omitted to get a licence from the king for operatic performances. George III had meanwhile transferred his support to a rival company in the Pantheon – no doubt to pique the Prince of Wales, who patronized Gallini. But Haydn remained stoical (helped no doubt by the fact that his fee for composing the opera had already been paid into his Viennese bank). On 14 March 1791 he wrote to Luigia Polzelli:

'Up to now our opera has not yet opened, and since the king won't give the licence, *Signor* Gallini intends to open it as if it were a subscription concert, for if he doesn't, he stands to lose twenty thousand pounds Sterling. I shan't lose anything, because the bankers Fries in Vienna have already received my money. My opera, entitled *L'Anima del filosofo*, will be staged at the end of May . . . Only our *prima donna* is a silly goose, and I shan't use her in my opera. We now await a yes or a no from the king, and if our theatre is opened, the other theatre, that is, our rivals, will have to close their doors, because the castrato and the *prima donna* are too old, and their opera didn't please anyone.'   (CCLN 115–16)

But when the opera had been completed and was actually in rehearsal, the blow fell:

'The Theatre now stood, completed, and the orchestra was gathered together to rehearse the opera *Orfeo*. Haydn had distributed the parts, and hardly were forty bars played through, when persons in authority entered and in the name

* Who fell in love with Dussek and married him the next year: she was 16, he was 30.

34

of king and parliament forbade the opera to take place in any fashion whatsoever, not even in the form of a rehearsal. *Orfeo* was, as it were, declared to be contraband, and the worst of it was that the performance of *all* operas in the Theatre was forbidden for the future.' (Dies: Landon 71)

'Sir John' Gallini eventually recovered the licence, but too late for Haydn's opera, which was shelved, unstaged; its first complete performance was given in Florence in 1951!

A series of happier events, however, overtook these operatic misfortunes. The first of these, Haydn's Benefit Concert, was announced for 16 May.

HANOVER-SQUARE
MR HAYDN'S NIGHT
MAY the 16th 1791

PART THE FIRST	PART THE SECOND
New Grand Overture – HAYDN	*By particular Desire* the New Grand Overture, *Haydn*, as performed at Mr Salomon's first Concert
Aria – Signora STORACE	
Concertante for two Corni Bassetti, Messrs SPRINGER and DWORSACK	Cantata – Signor PACCHIEROTTI – Haydn
New Aria, with Oboe and Bassoon obligati, Signor DAVID – *Haydn*	Concertante for Piano Forte and Pedal Harp, Mr DUSSECK, and Madame KRUMPHOLTZ
Concerto, Violin Mr GIORNOVICHII	Ductto – Sig. DAVID and Sig. PACCHIEROTTI

Finale – HAYDN

'Haydn's Benefit proved so completely crowded, that during the evening his *own* were the only movements practicable' (*The Times*); £200 had been guaranteed by Salomon, £350 was actually taken (for which Haydn courteously thanked the public in the next day's paper).

The final week of May found Haydn attending a 'Grand Music Meeting' in Westminster Abbey – the Handel Festival given by over a thousand performers. William

OPERA HOUSE OR KING'S THEATRE IN THE HAY-MARKET

Gardiner,* an enthusiastic amateur musician from Leicester, was in the audience, and through a telescope observed Haydn placed near the 'double bass Kettle drums'. It was probably from this vantage point that Haydn acquired the following *Anectod*:

'Just as the director of a grand concert was about to begin the first number, the kettledrummer called loudly to him and said he should wait a moment, since his 2 kettledrums were not yet tuned. The leader could and would not wait any longer, and said he should transpose in the meantime.'

(CCLN 259)

The last of Salomon's concerts took place on 3 June, and Haydn's friends set about devising ways of continuing his attachment to England. An academic distinction would add emphasis to the hopes (already expressed in print after the first of Salomon's concerts) that Haydn would eventually take up his residence in that country, and an honorary

* This same Gardiner will be supplying us with our final Footnote.

doctorate was proposed at Oxford University. *Jackson's Oxford Journal* had begun the year auspiciously by declaring that 'Italian Singers – German Music – French Dancers – Swiss Servants – and Spanish Paint – are the fashionable things of this winter', and although, in the spring, Haydn had failed to appear at an Oxford concert for which he had been billed as the 'attraction of the evening', by the summer he was again 'this musical Shakespeare – this musical Draw-cansir,* who can equal the strains of a Cherub, and enchant in all the gradations between those and a ballad'. Dies gives us a composite account from his researches and Haydn's own words:

'Dr Burney was the moving spirit: he talked Haydn into it and went with him to Oxford. At the ceremony in the University Hall, the assembled company was encouraged to present the doctor's hat to a man who had risen so high in the service of music. The whole company was loud in Haydn's praises. Thereupon Haydn was presented with a white silk gown, the sleeves in red silk, and a little black hat, and thus arrayed, he had to seat himself in a doctor's chair . . . Haydn

* A curious metaphor. Drawcansir is the blustering bully in Buckingham's *Rehearsal* who 'kills 'em all on both sides'.

HAYDN'S THANKS TO THE ENGLISH PUBLIC

MR. HAYDN, extremely flattered with his reception in a Country which he had long been ambitious of visiting, and penetrated with the patronage with which he has been honoured by its animated and generous Inhabitants, should think himself guilty of the greatest ingratitude, if he did not take the earliest opportunity of making his most grateful Acknowledgements to the English Public in general, as well as to his particular Friends, for the zeal which they have manifested at his CONCERT, which has been supported by such distinguished marks of favour and approbation, as will be remembered by him with infinite delight as long as he lives.

was asked to present something of his own composition. He climbed up to the organ loft, turned to the company, took his doctorial robes in both hands, opened them at his breast, closed them again and said as loudly and clear as possible (in English), "I thank you." The company well understood this unexpected gesture; they appreciated Haydn's thanks and said, "You speak very good English." "I felt very silly in my gown, and the worst of it was, I had to drag it round the streets for three whole days. But I have much to thank this doctor's degree in England; indeed, I might say everything; as a result of it, I gained the acquaintance of the first men in the land and had entrance to the greatest houses."'

(Dies: Landon 71)

The three days were filled with musical presentations in the Sheldonian Theatre, reported, with all their vicissitudes, by the London press. The first concert was beset with travelling difficulties which afflicted not only Haydn himself, but also the leading vocalist, Mrs Crouch, who was

'unfortunately taken dangerously ill on the road, with a sore throat and violent fever. She was left under proper care at Henley, and a physician was despatched to her from Oxford . . .

'A New M.S. Overture by Haydn, was to have introduced the Second Act; but as Haydn did not reach Oxford [in] time enough for a rehearsal, one of his former pieces was the substitute, and the Composer himself sat at the Organ . . .'   (*Morning Herald* 8.vii.91)

Although it would not have been unusual at this period to perform a piece unrehearsed, we know Haydn's feelings on the matter from another occasion that he thought important enough to record in the Notebook:

'I was invited by Dr Arnold and his associates to a grand concert in Free Maisons Hall: one of my big symphonies was to have been given under my direction, but since they wouldn't have any rehearsal, I refused to cooperate and did not appear.'   (CCLN 289)

On the second day in Oxford, although 'Mrs Crouch remains in such a dangerous state at Henley, that all hope of her assistance was relinquished . . . The new Overture of Haydn, prepared for the occasion, and previously rehearsed in the morning, led on the second Act, and a more wonderful composition never was heard.' (*Morning Herald* 9.vii.91)

This was the 'Oxford' symphony, No. 92 in G.

On 8 July the concluding concert took place; the Sheldonian Theatre was 'prodigiously hot'. In the first act was

'a beautiful Cantata by Haydn, who appeared in his gown and conducted it; – this charming air used to be finely sung by Marches; therefore Storace was injudicious in attempting it on this occasion, and indeed, obtained less applause than Haydn's *Doctorial Robe*.

'A new Overture by Pleyel led on the second act. The composition was much admired and the Band played it with very great correctness and spirit, though they never saw it till that evening.

'Kelly before the third act sung an Italian Air, the music of which was not very striking; and he made as much of it as it deserved.

'The last act commenced with an Overture of Haydn, very fine, but well known.

'When the performers quitted the Orchestra, they were severally greeted with much applause. It seemed to be the general opinion, that no performance at this place ever went with better success. The company were said to exceed the number of visitors usually present for many years.'

(*Morning Herald* 11.vii.91)

We are relieved to be told, as an afterthought, that 'Mrs Crouch who continues at Henley, is pronounced out of danger, and the merit of her recovery is attributed to Dr Hall of Oxford.' (*Morning Herald* 11.vii.91)

Haydn's Notebook account of the three days, though mis-spelt, is more succinct:

'I had to pay $1\frac{1}{2}$ guineas for having the bells rung at Oxforth

39

in connection with my doctor's degree, and $\frac{1}{2}$ a guinea for the robe. The trip cost 6 guineas.' (CCLN 274)

Oxford was the first real expedition that Haydn had made from London, but now, with the concert season over, he was at liberty at last to accept the invitations which had been accumulating. Prudence prompted him to spend some time in seclusion, composing the new set of symphonies for the next season, and also adding to his already considerable bank balance by giving piano lessons. 'Every lesson was paid for with a guinea', he noted in surprise.

'Mrs Schroeter presents her compliments to Mr Haydn, and informs him, she is just returned to town, and will be very happy to see him whenever it is convenient to him to give her a lesson.

James St: Buckingham gate Wednesday
June the 29th $\overline{791}$' (CCLN 279)

Of this pupil we shall hear more later on; for the moment Haydn preferred the countryside to Buckingham Gate, and accepted an invitation from the banker Nathaniel Brassey to stay with him and his family in their country house near Hertford. 'Stayed there 5 weeks. I was very well entertained', he noted, and wrote back to Maria Anna von Genzinger in Vienna on 17 September 1791:

'I have been living in the country, amid the loveliest scenery, with a banker's family where I live as if I were in a monastery. I am all right, thank the good Lord! except for my usual rheumatism; I work hard, and when in the early mornings I walk in the woods, alone, with my English grammar, I think of my Creator, my family, and all the friends I have left behind. How sweet this bit of freedom really is! I had a kind prince, but sometimes I was forced to be dependent on base souls. I often sighed for release, and now I have it in some measure. I appreciate the good sides of all this, too, though my mind is burdened with far more work. The realization that I am no bond-servant makes ample amends for all my toils. But, dear though this liberty is to me, I should like to enter Prince Esterházy's service again when I return, if only for the sake of my family.' (CCLN 118)

Only one incident disturbed the rural peace, and that appears to have been brought on by Haydn himself telling anecdotes of the earlier and less fortunate times of his life.

'Haydn and [Brassey] were once together, and the latter listened attentively to such an anecdote. Suddenly he jumped up like a madman, yelling the most frightful curses, and swearing that he would kill himself on the spot if he had loaded pistols.

'Haydn meanwhile had also got up and yelled for help. "Just don't shoot me!" He thought he had only one life, and it seemed to him that it was too soon to lose it.

'The banker's wife and other people rushed, horrified, to the scene. The banker roared at them, "Pistols! I'm going to shoot myself." The people were shaking but tried to calm him down and find out why he had developed those murderous instincts. The banker refused for a long time to give any answer, until finally they asked him with tears in their eyes. Then he repeated the violent oaths and said he wanted to shoot himself because he never knew trouble, misery and poverty; and as he now realized he was not really happy, for all he knew how to do was to stuff himself and drink; he had been surrounded with plenty, and it now disgusted him.'

(Dies: Landon 96)

We may take it that the banker did not shoot himself, because Haydn, with characteristic *sang froid*, later reduced the incident in his Notebook to:

'N.B.: Herr Brassy once cursed, because he had had too easy a time in this world.' (CCLN 271)

Another country expedition was to Suffolk to stay for a few days with Sir Patrick Blake and his wife. By taking a devious route Haydn managed to see 'the little town of Cambridge'.

'Saw the universities there, which are very conveniently situated, one after another, in a row, but each one separate from the other; each university has at the back of it a very roomy and beautiful garden, besides beautiful stone bridges, in order to be able to cross the circumjacent stream. The King's Chapel is famous because of its stuccoed ceiling. It is all made of stone, but so delicate that nothing more beautiful could have been made of wood. It is already 400 years old,* and everyone thinks that it is not more than 10 years old, because of the firmness and peculiar whiteness of the stone. The students there bear themselves like those at Oxford, but it is said that they have better teachers. There are in all 800 students.'   (CCLN 272)

Most glamorous of all his trips to country houses was one to Oatlands Park, near Walton-on-Thames, an extravagant mansion in a setting that impressed Haydn as much as it had the painter Farington, who noted:

'I have seen few situations more beautiful than the line of ground which is called the Terrace, and great taste has been shown in whatever has been done by the hand of Art. A large piece of made water, broad as a fine River, is directed in such a way as to appear to be part of the Thames although it has no connexion with it. Above the two ends, where it is lost in wood, the real River appears over the trees, and the imagination readily connects them. A lofty and well designed Temple is erected on the Terrace but is not finished, which is to be lamented as it would make a fine & proper object in this situation, and the view from it most beautiful & extensive.

'The House at Oatlands makes no appearance equal to the scenery about it, but being in a great measure hidden among trees, it does not become an object of much notice.'   (Farington I 77)

But for Haydn it was the company rather than the setting that roused his enthusiasm, as he wrote to Maria Anna von Genzinger on 20 December 1791:

'. . . 3 weeks ago I was invited by the Prince of Wales to visit his brother, the Duke of York, at the latter's country seat. The prince presented me to the duchess, the daughter of the

---

* For once Haydn gets his figures wrong; the Chapel was finished in 1515.

King of Prussia, who received me very graciously and said many flattering things. She is the most delightful lady in the world, is very intelligent, plays the pianoforte and sings very nicely. I had to stay there 2 days, because a slight indisposition prevented her attending the concert on the first day. On the 2nd day, however, she remained continually at my side from 10 o'clock in the evening, when the music began, to 2 o'clock in the morning. Nothing but Haydn was played. I conducted the symphonies from the pianoforte, and the sweet little thing sat beside me on my left and hummed all the pieces from memory, for she had heard them so often in Berlin. The Prince of Wales sat on my right side and played with us on his violoncello, quite tolerably. I had to sing, too. The Prince of Wales is having my portrait painted just now, and the picture is to hang in his room. The Prince of Wales is the most handsome man on God's earth; he has an extraordinary love of music and a lot of feeling, but not much money.'   (CCLN 122–3)

The portrait of Haydn was painted by John Hoppner, who was chosen by the Prince of Wales – possibly to pique his father. George III wasted little affection on 'Prinny', and was also critical of Hoppner's colouring to his face. According to Farington,

OATLANDS PARK, SURREY

'When the King said He did not approve of red & yellow trees and that artists shd. look at nature, Hoppner said He had studied landscape as much as anybody. When the King directed his discourse to any other person present Hoppner replied as if He had been the person spoken to. He looked white & was much agitated. After the King left the room, Hoppner spoke very passionately . . . He said He did not come there to solicit employment and that He knew He was the best Painter in England.'   (Farington II 376)

Possibly Haydn found Hoppner as truculent as the king did. Legend has it that his expression during the sittings was so unsmiling that a German serving-maid had to be produced to engage him in diversionary German conversation before a likeness could be caught!

From the charms of Oatlands it must have been a rude shock for Haydn to be back in the frenzy of the London concert world, installed once more in central lodgings, which he shared with Salomon, in Great Pulteney Street.

The plethora of festivities peculiar to the English autumn overwhelmed him, and his incomplete understanding of them must have left him somewhat perplexed at the bizarre ways of the English: 'On 5th Nov. the boys celebrate the days on which the Guys set the town on fire.'   (CCLN 268)

But on the same day that such arcane activities were taking place outside, he was invited to the Lord Mayor's Banquet in the Guildhall, where he found neither the music nor the English drinking habits particularly edifying. It is passages like this that make one wish Haydn had spread himself more frequently when reporting on the English.

'The new Lord Mayor and his wife ate at the first table No. 1, then the Lord Chanceler and both the Scherifs, Duc de Lids [Leeds], Minuster Pitt and the other judges of the first rank. At No. 2 I ate with Mr Silvester, the greatest lawyer and first Alderman of London. In this room (which is called the geld Hall) there were 16 tables besides others in adjoining rooms; in all nearly 1200 persons dined, all with the greatest pomp. The food was very nice and well-cooked; many kinds of wine in abundance. The company sat down at 6 o'clock and arose at 8. The Lord Mayor was escorted according to rank before and also after dinner, and there were many ceremonies, a sword was carried in front of him, and a kind of golden crown, to the sound of trumpets, accompanied by a wind band. After dinner the distinguished company of [table] No. 1 retired to a separate room which had been chosen beforehand, to drink coffee and tea; we other guests, however, were taken to another adjoining room. At 9 o'clock No. 1 rose and went to a small room, at which point the ball began: in this room there is, *a parte*, an elevated place for the high *Nobless* where the Lord Mayor is seated on a throne together with his wife. Then the dancing begins according to rank, but only 1 couple, just as at Court on the King's Birthday, 6th January. In this small room there are 4 tiers of raised benches on each side, where the fair sex mostly has the upper hand. Nothing but minuets are danced in this room; I couldn't stand it longer than a quarter of an hour; first, because the heat caused by so many people in such a small room was so great; and secondly, because of the wretched dance band, the entire orchestra consisting only of two violins and a violoncello. The minuets were more Polish than in our or the Italian manner. From there I went to another room, which was more like a subterranean cavern, and where the dance was English; the music was a little better, because there was a drum in the band which drowned the misery of the violins. I went on to the great hall, where we had eaten, and there the band was larger and more bearable. The dance was English, but only on the raised platform where the Lord Mayor and the first 4 numbers had dined; the other tables, however, were all occupied again by men who, as usual, drank enormously the whole night. The most curious thing, though, is that a part of the company went on dancing without hearing a single note of the music, for first at one table, then at another, some were yelling songs and some swilling it down and drinking toasts amid terrific roars of "Hurrey, H[urrey], H[urrey]" and waving of glasses. The hall and all the other rooms are illuminated with lamps which give out an unpleasant odour. It is remarkable that the Lord Mayor requires no knife at table, for a carver, who

45

stands in front of him in the middle of the table, cuts up everything for him in advance.

'Behind the Lord Mayor there is another man who, as is the custom, shouts out all the toasts as loudly as he can; after each shout come fanfares of trumpets and kettledrums. No toast was more applauded than that of Mr Pitt. But otherwise there is no order. This dinner cost £1600; half must be paid by the Lord Mayor, the other half by the two Sherifs. The Lord Mayor is newly elected every year. He wears, over his costume, a large black satin mantle, long and wide, in the shape of a domino cloak, richly ornamented in gold lace bands, especially round the arms. Round his neck he wears a large gold chain like that of our *Toison Order*; his wife has the same, she is Mylady and remains so. A new one is elected every year. The whole ceremony is worth seeing, especially the procession up the Tems from Guildhall to Westmynster.' (CCLN 251–3)

Four weeks later, as the days drew in and the weather deteriorated, Haydn noted: 'On 5th Dec. the fog was so thick that you could have spread it on bread. In order to write I had to light the lights at 11 o'clock.' (CCLN 278)

On the same night Mozart died in Vienna. The news took several weeks to reach London, and when it did Haydn could only bring himself to make the briefest of notes: 'Mozard starb den 5^{tn} 10^{bri} 1791 [Mozart died the 5th of December 1791].' (Landon 113)

Haydn was deeply upset by the news, and never relinquished his view that 'Mozart was the greatest musical genius that ever existed'. He had walked arm-in-arm with him to the rehearsals of *Così Fan Tutte*, he had played in quartet parties with him. The two composers had been like brothers. Haydn wrote emotionally, but also with practical suggestions, to Mozart's fellow Mason in Vienna, Johann Michael Puchberg, in January 1792:

'. . . For some time I was beside myself about his death, and I could not believe that Providence would so soon claim the life of such an indispensable man. I only regret that before his death he could not convince the English, who walk in darkness in this respect, of his greatness – a subject about which I have been sermonizing to them every single day . . . You will be good enough, my kind friend, to send me a catalogue of those pieces which are not yet known here, and I shall make every possible effort to promote such works for the widow's benefit.' (CCLN 125)

In his encyclopedia article on Mozart Charles Burney gives first-hand evidence that Haydn was as good as his word.

'When Haydn was asked in our hearing by Broderip, in his music-shop whether Mozart had left any MS. compositions behind him that were worth purchasing, as his widow had offered his unedited papers at a high price to the principal publishers of music through-out Europe; Haydn eagerly said: "Purchase them by all means. He was truly a great musician. I have been often flattered by my friends with having some genius; but he was much my superior." ' (Rees)

Salomon had had the initiative, at that final dinner party in Vienna when he collected Haydn, to make a similar arrangement with Mozart to visit England the season after Haydn left. Haydn had found the sequence very proper, for, as he said, if Mozart had gone first there would have been no point in his following, since 'nothing would do after Mozart's compositions'.

Curiously, though, many of Mozart's compositions were already to be heard in England, but often presented anonymously. That very English form of 'operatick' entertainment, the ballad-opera, had developed into the pantomime opera and the 'after-piece', the delight of the patrons of the two London opera houses. But these works, attributed to the pens of Shield, Storace, Arnold and many other indefatigable labourers in London's entertainment business, were in fact 'compiled' more often than 'composed'. *Prima donnas* (even English-born) would claim their right to insert into any new production their favourite arias from Paisiello, Gluck, Boyce, Geminiani or, in fact, any ballad-tune with which they had previously made a hit. The return of Stephen

47

Storace and his sister Nancy from Vienna (where they had worked with Mozart, Nancy as the first Susanna in *Figaro*) meant a steady supply of Mozart arias, usually in manuscript. Michael Kelly,* the entertaining Irish singer and 'composer' who had sung Don Basilio for Mozart, was also back in town, together with Mozart's young English pupil, Thomas Attwood. Not surprisingly, extracts from *Figaro*, and even *The Magic Flute*, first reached the ears of English theatre-goers in confections with titles such as *The Prisoner*, *Osmyn and Daraxa* and (appropriately) *The Pirates*.

Haydn's own music was also appropriated in this way, as we shall see, in the following year. For the moment, though, he could attend the theatre without contributing to the entertainment, but, as ever, with an eye for local peculiarities and statistics, which he noted methodically.

'Before she left for Italy, Mara sang 4 times at the Heymarcket Theatre in the English opera *Artaxerses* by Dr Arnd [Arne]. Again she won roars of applause, and she was paid £100 for each appearance.' (CCLN 277)

'Heymarket Theatre
It holds 4,000 persons; the pit, or parterre, alone holds 1,200; 10 persons can sit comfortably in each box. The *Amphy Theater* is entirely round, it has four tiers, and to light it there is a beautiful large chandelier with 70 lights: it hangs suspended from the attic, pierces the ceiling, and is situated in the middle of the *Amphy Theater;* it illuminates the whole house, but there are also *a parte* small lustres in the first and 2nd tiers, which are fastened outside the boxes half an ell away.' (CCLN 274)

'English Fanaticism. Miss Dora Jordan, a mistress of the Duc de Clarens [Clarence] and the leading actress at Drury Lane, wrote to the impresario one evening, an hour before the beginning of a comedy in which she was to play, that she had been taken ill suddenly and therefore couldn't act. When the curtain was raised in order to inform the public

* When he later ran a wine business, Sheridan suggested that his title should be 'Compiler of Wines and Importer of Music'.

thereof, and to say that the management was inclined to give another piece, the whole public began to shout that the comedy which had been announced must be given at once, with another actress taking Jordan's rôle and reading with the part in her hand. At the beginning, the management took exception to this plan, but the public became stubborn and its wishes had to be satisfied. Miss Jordan made herself contemptible in the public's eyes because she drove bare-facedly in Heÿ [Hyde] Park with the Duc. But she begged for pardon in all the newspapers, and people quite forgave her.' (CCLN 278)

'Covent-garden is the National Theatre. I was there on 10th Dec. and saw an opera called *The Woodman*. It was the very day on which the life story of Madam Bilington, both from the good as well as from the bad sides, was announced; such impertinent enterprises are generally undertaken for [selfish] interests. She sang rather timidly this evening, but very well all the same. The first tenor [Charles Incledon] has a good voice and quite a good style, but he uses the falsetto to excess. He sang a trill on high C and ran up to G. The 2nd tenor tries to imitate him, but could not make the change from the falsetto to the natural voice, and apart from that he is most unmusical. He creates a new tempo for himself, now 3/4, then 2/4, makes cuts whenever it occurs to him. But the cahest [cast] is entirely used to him. The leader is Herr Baumgartner, a German who, however, has almost forgotten his mother-tongue. The Theatre is very dark and dirty, and is almost as large as the Vienna Court Theatre. The common people in the galleries of all the theatres are very impertinent; they set the fashion with all their unrestrained impetuosity, and whether something is repeated or not is determined by their yells. The parterre and all the boxes sometimes have to applaud a great deal to have something good repeated. That was just what happened this evening, with the Duet in the 3rd Act, which was very beautiful; and the pro's and contra's went on for nearly a quarter of an hour, till finally the parterre and the boxes won, and they repeated the Duet. Both the performers stood on the stage

quite terrified, first retiring, then again coming forward. *The orchestra is sleepy.*' (CCLN 273–4)

The Woodman was composed by William Shield, but as one might have expected, the 'very beautiful duet' was not the product of Shield at all, but came from Boyce's *Solomon*. As an indication of the commercial prospects of this type of patch-work, Longman bought *The Woodman* from Shield for publication for 1000 guineas.*

The full story of Mrs Billington's misdemeanours (the 'good side' hardly features) eventually reached the public in January of 1792, but not before the publisher had extracted the maximum publicity from the impending embarrassment of this great soprano. As a singer, according to Burney,

'the natural tone of her voice is exquisitely sweet, her knowledge of music so considerable, her shake so true, her closes and embellishments so various, and her expression so grate-

---

* This may have been overgenerous, since Longman went into bankruptcy three years later.

ful, that nothing but envy and apathy can hear her without delight.' (Burney II 1021)

She had a brilliant coloratura and a range up to G in alt that exceeded the Queen of the Night by a whole tone. The only whiff of professional criticism was that, according to Anthony Pasquin,

> *She oft wants the gentle assistance of ease,*
> *And seems more intent to surprise than to please.*
>
> 'The Children of Thespis' (London 1786–8)

Her private life was a different matter; whatever pleasures she had given (or taken), the surprise at their publication moved even Haydn, used though he was to the licence allowed a great singer, to comment:

'Today, 14 January 1792, the life of Madam Bilingthon was published in print. Her life is exposed in the most shameless detail. The publisher is said to have got hold of her own letters, and to have offered to return them to her for 10 guineas; otherwise he intended to print them publicly. But she didn't want to spend the 10 guineas, and demanded her letters through the courts; she was refused, whereupon she appealed, but in vain; for even though her opponent offered her £500, he nevertheless issued this treasure of hers today, and you couldn't get a single copy after 3 o'clock in the afternoon.

'It is said that her character is the worst sort, but that she is a great genius, and all the women hate her because she is so beautiful. N.B. She is said, however, to have written the most scandalous letters, containing accounts of her amours, to her mother. She is said to be an illegitimate child, and it's even believed that her own supposed father is involved in this affair.

'Such stories are common in London. The husband provides opportunities for his wife so that he can profit from it, whereby he relieves his "brother-in-law" of £1000 Sterling and more.' (CCLN 255)

One does wonder whether Haydn contented himself with 'it is said', or whether his curiosity did not lead him to read this scurrilous pamphlet in more detail. The instigator of the scandal, one John Ridgeway, claimed to be offering 'Memoirs of Mrs Billington . . . containing a variety of matters, Ludicrous, Theatrical, Musical, and —', but it was the final, unnameable category that made up most of the volume, soft pornography couched uncomfortably in musical terminology.

'The instrument which James Billington, *very ably, and harmoniously had been accustomed to perform upon*, was a REMARKABLE GOOD TENOR. He attempted a *little flute*, for the first time, the *same day* he was married, and again the *next morning*; but it was so defective in its *construction*, that his wife insisted he should *put it up*, and she has never permitted him to *perform* with it since.

'As the lady is unquestionably a good musician, it is not to be wondered at, if I declare that there is no woman more capable of determining in an instant upon the *tone* or *construction* of any instrument: her *feeling* is exquisite, and her musical knowledge in general, second to none, not even to the *judgment* of Mrs Jordan or Mrs Crouch, upon *any* instrument.

'Soon after her marriage, Billington, his wife, her father and brother, went to Ireland upon an engagement with Mr Daly, to *perform* in Dublin; and as I shall have occasion soon to mention the name of CRAY, a Gentleman, who was remarkable for his *performances* upon a musical instrument almost *peculiar* to that enviable nation, I shall describe it!

'It was called a *Celestina*, exactly of the *shape* and *make* of a DOUBLE BASSOON, which by the improvement and addition of a large END or TOP, could be tuned to the greatest nicety, in the same manner as the improved German Flutes, by pulling out the end, or putting it in close. From the delicate ear of Mrs Billington, she could always keep it in tune, by a shifting movement, which she applied to the instrument, at pleasure. This instrument is particularly constructed, and is played in pieces of music set in *Two Parts*, or *Duets*, but the manner of holding the instrument, being somewhat singular, I must be under the necessity of describing the manner in which it is played upon. Place the instrument horizontally, the end or top in a strait line, by which means you have command of it, and of course can change the time, according as the music varies. It succeeds best in such music in which the time is progressive: for instance, if the bar you begin with is a *Breve*, which is the longest note in music, you get a pause or rest of the same measure, and so on, occasioned by the different measures of the notes before you. It is harmonious and pleasing in any time, or in any key, but it is exquisitely so when you come to quick time, which is the measure most delectable upon the *Celestina*. The music written in common time for this instrument has a long pause, or Ad Libitum mark ⌒, which must be dwelt upon, before you can *Da Capo*. Once when Mr Cray was performing upon this double basse, or Celestina, accompanied by Mrs Billington upon the Piano Forte, by the effort he made to produce a fine effect, her instrument being perfectly in tune, the maid, who was likewise fond of *music*, upon hearing a *great crash* of the instruments, ran into the room, and found her mistress's piano forte, had given way, by the breaking of one of the jacks. This accident brought upon Mrs Billington a dreadful illness, when after trying every remedy, recommended by the faculty in such cases, she had at last the happiness to experience a perfect cure, by taking some bottles of Velnos' Vegetable Syrup, prepared by Mr Swainson, Frith-street, Soho.'

Even though the 'affaire Billington' may well have confirmed him in his opinion that English women 'stay whores all their lives', it is reassuring to note that even at the height of the scandal Haydn was never deflected in his admiration for Mrs Billington as a singer, and simply apportioned the blame to those who profited from the affair. Nor was there ever a breath of impropriety to touch Haydn during all his time in England.

But at this juncture Mrs Billington's misfortunes were forgotten in the sudden outbreak of musical hostilities that burst upon Haydn, and even a temper as equable as his found it hard to tolerate the machinations of the musical factions at work in the concert world. Most painful of all, he found his own pupil and protégé, Ignaz Pleyel, employed to work against him.

The rival faction to Salomon and his concert series in the Hanover Square Rooms was The Professional Concert, also held in the Hanover Square Rooms, but on Tuesdays. They, in fact, had boasted the attraction of Mrs Billington, and, having failed to attract Haydn to England some years earlier, went out of their way to undermine him in the press. Immediately after his arrival with Salomon the campaign had started:

'Upon the arrival of Haydn, it was discovered that he no longer possessed his former powers. Pity it is that the discovery did not possess the merit of novelty. What less could have been expected from his presence?'

(*Morning Chronicle* 13.i.91)

The rival series immediately championed the symphonies of his pupil:

'His pupil Pleyel, with perhaps less science, is a more popular composer – from his more frequent introduction of *air* into his *harmonies*, and the general smoothness of his melodies.'   (*Gazetteer* 5.ii.91)

With the opening of Salomon's series, this innuendo was soon seen to be baseless – Haydn's genius-box, to the relief of the Rev. Twining, was found to be bottomless – and the opposition was dimmed. But only for the moment. If the presence of Pleyel's music was not sufficient, then they would bring over the composer himself for the next season. Thus we find Haydn, ingenuous as ever, noting: 'On 23rd Dec. Pleyel arrived in London. On the 24th I dined with him.'   (CCLN 274)

Harmonious relations were established, as the *Public Advertiser* on 5 January so solicitously wished:

'Haydn and Pleyel are to be *pitted* against each other this season; and the supporters of each are violent partizans. As both these Composers are men of first-rate talents, it may be hoped that they will not participate in the little feelings of their respective admirers.'   (*Public Advertiser* 5.i.92)

PLEYEL

However, Burney had predicted the previous year, 'It will be a busy & memorable season in the Hist^y of Tweedle-dum and Tweedle-dee Quarrels', and the relative merits of the two protagonists, both of them negotiated into positions they would rather have avoided, were loudly rehearsed in the press. The 'Off' was announced in February 1792:

Mr SALOMON'S CONCERT
HANOVER-SQUARE

MR SALOMON most respectfully acquaints the Nobility and Gentry, that his Concert will open on Friday, the 17th instant, and continuing on the succeeding Friday, upon the same grand scale as last year.

Dr Haydn, who is engaged for the whole Season, will give every night a New Piece of his Composition, and direct the Performance of it at the Piano Forte.   (*Oracle* 13.i.92)

PROFESSIONAL CONCERT,
HANOVER-SQUARE

The Committee respectfully acquaint the Subscribers, that

55

the FIRST CONCERT will be on Monday next, February the 13th.

ACT I
Overture – HAYDN
Song – Signor LAZZARINI
Concert Violin – Mr CRAMER
Song – Mrs BILLINGTON
Grand Symphony, composed for the occasion, Mr PLEYEL

ACT II
Concerto Violoncello – Mr LINDLEY
Song – Signora NEGRI
Concerto French Harp – Madame MUSEGNY
Duetto – Signor LAZZARINI and Mrs BILLINGTON
Symphony MOZART

(*Morning Herald* 9.ii.92)

Haydn's letters to Vienna during this period tell of the strain he was under from this competitive atmosphere; in conditions quite unlike any he had ever encountered before, he was still prepared to over-work himself in order to do the best he could for his friend Salomon.

Haydn to Polzelli (his mistress) in Vienna, 14 January:

'I have a lot to do, especially now, when the Professional Concert has had my pupil Pleyel brought over, to face me as a rival; but I'm not afraid, because last year I made a great impression on the English and hope therefore to win their approval this year, too. My opera was not given, because *Sig.* Gallini didn't receive the licence from the king, and never will; to tell you the truth, the Italian opera has no success at all now, and by a stroke of bad luck, the Pantheon Theatre burned down just this very day, two hours after midnight.

'I am quite well, but am almost always in an "English humour", that is depressed, and perhaps I shall never again regain the good humour that I used to have when I was with you. Oh! my dear Polzelli: you are always in my heart, and I shall never, never forget you.' (CCLN 126)

Haydn to Maria Anna von Genzinger in Vienna, 17 January:

'. . . if Your Grace could only see how I am tormented, here in London, by having to attend all sorts of private concerts, which cause me great loss of time; and by the vast amount of work which has been heaped on my shoulders, you would, my gracious Lady, have the greatest pity on me. I never in my life wrote so much in one year as I have here during this past one, but now I am almost completely exhausted, and it will do me good to be able to rest a little when I return home. At present I am working for Salomon's concerts, and I am making every effort to do my best, because our rivals, the Professional Concert, have had my pupil Pleyel from Strassburg come here to conduct their concerts. So now a bloody harmonious war will commence between master and pupil. The newspapers are all full of it, but it seems to me that there will soon be an armistice, because my reputation is so firmly established here. Pleyel behaved so modestly towards me upon his arrival that he won my affection again. We are very often together, and this does him credit, for he knows how to appreciate his father. We shall share our laurels equally and each go home satisfied.'   (CCLN 128)

But while he was writing these letters, Haydn was receiving a simultaneous sequence from nearer home, in which we can trace the development of an attachment which must have served to restore him emotionally over these trying months. These letters came from Rebecca Schroeter, the piano pupil who had presented her compliments to Haydn the previous summer. She was the widow of Johann Schroeter, the successor to John Christian Bach as Music Master to the queen, who had died three years before Haydn came to London.

Rebecca Schroeter Burney described as 'a young lady of considerable fortune and . . . in easy circumstances'. Her growing affection for Haydn is obvious, but without any of Haydn's replies to her solicitous notes, it is difficult to know to what extent these feelings were reciprocated. We only have his remarks to his biographer Dies, made in old age, when confronted with the copies he had made of Mrs Schroeter's letters in his Notebooks (presumably because she had asked for the originals back):

'Haydn smiled and said: "Letters from an English widow in

London, who loved me; but she was, though already sixty years old,* still a beautiful and charming woman and I would have married her very easily if I had been free at the time."'   (Dies: Landon 87)

In his copies Haydn carefully preserved Mrs Schroeter's abbreviations: 'F' – Faithful; 'M.D.' – My Dear; 'D.' – Dear; 'Dst' – Dearest; 'M.Dst' – My Dearest; 'H' and 'Hn' – Haydn; 'D.H.' – Dear Haydn.

Rebecca Schroeter:

'Wednesday Feb: 8th, $\overline{7}$92.
M:D: Inclos'd I have Sent you the words of the Song you desired. – I wish much to know, *how you do* to day, I am very sorry to lose the pleasure of seeing you this morning, but I hope you will have time to come to morrow, I beg my D: you will take great care of your health, and do not fatigue yourself with to[o] much application to buss[i]ness. my thoughts and best wishes are always with you, and I ever am with the utmost Sincerity M:D your F: et[c].'   (CCLN 279)

Meanwhile the state of warfare can be deduced from the daily papers: despite the induced rivalry, each man featured the other's music in his concerts.

For example, *The Morning Chronicle*, 16 February:

Mr SALOMON'S CONCERT
HANOVER-SQUARE

Mr SALOMON most respectfully acquaints the Nobility and Gentry, that his first Concert will be Friday next, the 17th instant.

PART I
Overture, Pleyel
Song, Mr Nield
Concert Oboe, Mr Harrington
Song, Signor Calcagni, (being his first appearance in this Country)

---

* Dies, or Haydn, must have been mistaken here. She could have been sixty when the story was retold (in 1806) but not when they first met.

Concert Pedal Harp, Madame Delaval
Song, Miss Corri

PART II
New Grand Overture, Haydn
Song, Signor Calcagni
Concerto Violin, Mr Janieviez
Duetto, Miss Corri, and Mr Nield
Finale, Gyrowetz
The doors to be opened at Seven . . .

Haydn to Maria Anna von Genzinger in Vienna, 2 March:

'. . . but there isn't a day, not a single day, in which I am free
from work, and I shall thank the dear Lord when I can leave
London – the sooner the better. My labours have been
augmented by the arrival of my pupil Pleyel, whom the
Professional Concert have brought here. He arrived here
with a lot of new compositions, but they had been composed

FIRST NIGHT TICKET TO HANOVER SQUARE CONCERT

long ago; he therefore promised to present a new work every evening. As soon as I saw this, I realized at once that a lot of people were dead set against me, and so I announced publicly that I would likewise produce 12 different new pieces. In order to keep my word, and to support poor Salomon, I must be the victim and work the whole time. But I really do feel it. My eyes suffer the most, and I have many sleepless nights, though with God's help I shall overcome it all. The people of the Professional Concert wanted to put a spoke in my wheel, because I would not go over to them; but the public is just. I enjoyed a great deal of success last year, but still more this year. Pleyel's presumption is sharply criticized, but I love him just the same. I always go to his concerts, and am the first to applaud him.'   (CCLN 132)

The Times, 20 February:

SALOMON's CONCERT

'The first Subscription Concert took place last Friday, at Hanover Square.

'The established musical judges present all agreed that it went off with surprising effect and rigid exactness. No Band in the world can go better.

'A new Overture from the pen of the incomparable *Haydn*, formed one considerable branch of this stupendous musical tree.

'Such a combination of excellence was contained in every movement, as inspired all the performers as well as the audience with enthusiastic ardour.

'Novelty of idea, agreeable caprice, and whim combined with all *Haydn's* sublime and wonten grandeur, gave additional consequence to the *soul* and feelings of every individual present.

'The Critic's eye brightened with additional lustre – then was the moment that the great Painter might have caught – that, which cannot be thrown on the human frame, but on such rare and great occasions.'

Rebecca Schroeter (undated):

'I am just return'd from from [*sic*] the Concert, where I was very much charmed with your *delightful* and enchanting *compositions*, and your spirited and interesting performance of them, accept ten thousand thanks for the great pleasure, I *always* receive from your *incomparable Music*. My D: I intreat you to inform me, how you do, and if you get any *Sleep* to Night. I am *extremely anxious* about your health. I hope to hear a good account of it. God Bless you *my* H. come to me to morrow I shall be happy to see you both morning and Evening, I always am with the tenderest Regard my D: your

F: and aff.

Friday Night 12 o'Clock'   (CCLN 286)

Morning Herald, 29 February:

Mr SALOMON'S CONCERT
HANOVER-SQUARE

Mr SALOMON most respectfully acquaints the Nobility and Gentry, that his third Performance will be on FRIDAY, March 2.

PART I
New Overture, M. S. GYROWETZ
Song, Signor ALBERTARELLI
Quartetto for Clarinet, Violin, Tenor and Violoncello,
Messrs. HARTMAN, SALOMAN, HINDMARSH
and MENEL. – Michel
Song, Miss CORRI
Concerto Violoncello. Mr DAMER (Pleyel)
(Being his first appearance in this country.)

PART II
New Grand Overture M. S. HAYDN
Song, Signor CALCAGNI
Concerto Violin, Mr. YANIEWICZ
Terzetto, Signor CALCAGNI, Signor ALBERTARELLI
and Miss CORRI – Tarchi
FINALE

Haydn's Notebook:

'In the 3rd concert, the new Symphony in B♭ was given, and the first and last Allegros encort.'   (CCLN 276)

Samuel Wesley also remembered this concert, and Haydn's contribution to the symphony [No. 98]:

'His Performance on the Piano Forte, although not such as to stamp him a first rate artist upon that Instrument, was indisputably neat and distinct. In the Finale of one of his Symphonies is a Passage of attractive Brilliancy, which he has given to the Piano Forte, and which the Writer of this Memoir remembers him to have executed with the utmost Accuracy and Precision.' (Wesley f.70)

Rebecca Schroeter:

'March 7th $\overline{92}$
My D: I was extremely sorry to part with you so suddenly last Night, our conversation was particularly interesting and I had [a] thousand affectionate things to say to you, my heart *was* and is full of *tenderness* for you, but no language can express *half the Love* and *affection* I feel for you, you are *dearer to me every Day* of my life. I am very sorry I was so dull and stupid yesterday, indeed my *Dearest* it was nothing but my being indisposed with a cold occasion'd my Stupidity. I thank you a thousand times for your Concern for me, I am truly sensible of your goodness, and I assure you my D., if any thing had happened to trouble me, I wou'd have open'd my heart, I told you with the most perfect confidence, oh, how earnes[t]ly [I] wish to see you, I hope you will come to me to morrow. I shall be happy to see you both in the Morning and the Evening. God Bless you my love, my thoughts and best wishes ever accompany you, and I always am with the most sincere invariable Regard my D:
          your truly affectio[nate]
   My Dearest I can not be happy
till I see you if you know,
do, tell me, when you will come'   (CCLN 279)

Diary; or, Woodfall's Register, 17 March:

HANOVER SQUARE
'The fifth Performance of the Concerts, under the direction of SALOMON and HAYDN, was held at this place last night, and

a more delicious assemblage of harmonic excellencies, we never attended. . . .

'HAYDN appeared with usual *éclat*, for six of his own compositions were performed, and they were all character[i]zed by beauty, expression, and originality. Of these pieces, a Concertante, and the fine representation of harmony, entitled, THE STORM, were the most striking; but particularly the latter, which was alternately tremendous and delightful, according to the perdominance [*sic*] of the imitation hurricane, or the approaching calm . . .'

The Notebook stoically remarks: 'On 17th March 1792 I was bled in London.' (CCLN 275)

At the next Salomon concert, the new symphony was 'The Surprise', and the *Oracle* excelled itself in poetic imagery:

'The Second Movement was equal to the happiest of this great Master's conceptions. The surprise might not be unaptly likened to the situation of a beautiful Shepherdess who, lulled to slumber by the murmur of a distant Waterfall, starts alarmed by the unexpected firing of a fowling-piece. The flute obligato was delicious.' (*Oracle* 24.iii.92)

Haydn, in later years, claimed that it was the need to compete with the Professionals rather than to rouse his sleepy audience that had provoked the sudden *fortissimo* chord – and it is nice to hear that Pleyel was there to enjoy it. Griesinger writes:

'I asked once in jest if it were true that he wrote the Andante with the kettledrum beat in order to awaken the English public that had gone to sleep at his concert. "No," he answered me. "Rather it was my wish to surprise the public with something new, and to make a début in a brilliant manner so as not to be outdone by my pupil Pleyel, who at that time was engaged by an orchestra in London (in the year 1792) which had begun its concert series eight days before mine. The first *Allegro* of my symphony was received with countless bravos, but the enthusiasm reached its highest point in the *Andante with the kettledrum beat. Ancora, Ancora!* sounded from every throat, and even Pleyel complimented me on my idea."'

(Landon 150)

Rebecca Schroeter:
'My D: I am extremely sorry I can not have the pleasure of seeing you to morrow, as I am going to Blackheath. if you are not engaged this Evening I shou'd be very happy if you will do me the favor to com[e] to me – and I hope to have the happiness to see you on Saturday to dinner, my thoughts and tenderest affections are always with you and I ever am most truly my D. your F: and etc.
April 4th $\overline{92}$.'   (CCLN 280)

'My D: with this, you will receive the Soap, I beg you a thousand Pardons for not Sending it sooner, I know you will have the goodness to excuse me. – I hope to hear you are quite well, and have slept well – I shall be happy to see you, my D: as soon as possible. I shall be much obliged to you if you will do me the favor to send me twelve Tikets for your Concert, may all success attend you my ever D: H: that Night, and always, is the sincere and hearty wish of your
                                             Invariable and
                                             truly affectionate
James S:
Aprill 8th $\overline{792}$.'   (CCLN 280)

'M: D: I was extremely sorry to hear this morning that you was indisposed, I am told you was five hours at your Study's yesterday, indeed *my* D: L: I am afraid it will hurt you, why should you who have already produced so many *wonderful* and *charming* compositions, still fatigue yourself with such close application. I almost tremble for your health, let me prevail on you my *much-loved* H: not to keep to your Study's so long at *one time*, my D: *love* if you cou'd know how very precious your welfare is to me, I flatter myself you wou'd endeavor to preserve it, for my Sake, as well as *your own*. pray inform me how you do and how you have slept, I hope to see you to Morrow at the concert, and on Saturday. I shall be happy to see you here to dinner, in the mean time my D: my sincerest good wishes constantly attend you, and I ever am with the tenderest regard your most
J: S: Aprill the 19th $\overline{92}$'   (CCLN 281)

By now it seems that Haydn was so pushed for time that he even employed Mrs Schroeter as a music copyist:

'Aprill 24th $\overline{792}$

'My D.

I can not leave London without sending you a line to assure you my thoughts[,] my *best wishes* and tenderest affections will inseperably attend you till we meet again.

'The Bearer will also deliver you the March, I am verry sorry, I cou'd not write it sooner, nor better, but I hope my D: you will excuse it, and if it is not passable, I will send you the *Dear* original directly: if my H: wou'd employ me oftener to write Music I hope I shou'd improve, and I know I shou'd delight in the occupation, now *my* D:L: let me intreat you to take the greatest care of your *health* I hope to see you on Friday at the concert and on Saturday to dinner till when and ever I most sincerely am, and shall be your [etc.]'

(CCLN 281)

'M:D: I am very anxious to know *how you do*, and hope to hear you have been in good health ever since I saw you – as the time for your charming concert advances I feel myself more and more interested for your Success, and heartely WISH every thing may turn out to your Satisfaction, do me the favor to send me Six Tickets more. on Saturday my D:L I hope to see you to dinner, in the mean while, my thoughts, my best wishes, and tenderest affections, constantly attend you, and I ever am my D: H: most sincerely and aff. [etc.]
J: S: May the 2^{d} $\overline{792}$'

(CCLN 281–2)

The final pressure that reduced Haydn to working for five hours at a stretch was his forthcoming Benefit Concert, for which the faithful Mrs Schroeter now appears to have ordered a total of 18 tickets. Also present was Mrs Papendiek, and her entrance ticket has been preserved,* with the note on the reverse: 'Presented to Mrs Papendiek by Dr Hayden himself at which concert ye Dutchess of York was

---

* Reproduced on the front cover of this volume.

present for the first time in England & 1500 people entered the door.'*

Burney was also there (and surely the Rev. Twining?); he heard works 'such as were never heard before, of any *mortal's* production; of what Apollo & the Muses compose or perform we can only judge by such productions as these.'

(Lonsdale 355)

But the strain was beginning to tell on Haydn, despite (or even augmented by) the adulation, as he told Maria Anna von Genzinger on 24 April 1792:

'Despite great opposition and the musical enemies who are so much against me – all of whom, together with my pupil Pleyel, tried their very hardest to crush me, especially this Winter – I have gained (thank God!) the upper hand. But I must admit that with all this work I am quite exhausted and wearied, and look forward longingly to the peace which will soon be mine.'

(CCLN 134)

And, with some relief, he was soon able to note: 'On 18th May 1792, the last Salomon Concert was given at Hanover Square.'

(CCLN 278)

A few musical commitments still remained (mostly in return for favours received), and Mrs Schroeter's correspondence continued in high ardour. There was a benefit concert for Salomon on 21 May, which naturally found Haydn presiding at the pianoforte, and one for the singer Mara, who managed to include in her programme one vocal piece that took Haydn by surprise.

'On 1st June 1792 Mara gave her benefit concert. They played two of my Symphonies, and I accompanied her, all by myself at the pianoforte, in a very difficult English Aria by Purcell. The audience was very small.'

(CCLN 258–9)

The aria in question is identified in the *Morning Herald* of

---

* She had previously claimed that the Rooms were 'calculated to hold 800 persons exclusive of the performers'. Since the room measured 79 × 32 feet, there would now seem to have been little more than $1\frac{1}{2}$ square feet for each person!

2 June 1792 as 'From Rosy Bowers', 'an irregular, impassioned, and pathetic song'; we assume it went off without disaster, although the remainder of the concert was not without incident:

'Young MEYER gave a charming Harp Concerto of KRUMP-HOLTZ, with admirable skill, though under evident embarrassment from diffidence, and the vexation arising from the breaking of several strings.

'The other accidents of the evening, were the fall of an *infirm sopha*, and the consequent *prostration* of some *venerable beaux*, and the *lodgement* of a whole cupfull of hot tea down the neck of MARA, by the sudden movement of some awkward arm.'

Haydn obviously retired home out of sorts, and Mrs Schroeter enquired anxiously the next morning:

'My D^r I beg to know *how you do?* hope to hear you[r] Head-ach is *entirely gone*, and that you have *slept well*. I shall be very happy to see you on Sunday any time convenient to you after one o'Clock – I hope to see you my D^r L on tuesday as usual to *Dinner*, and all [night?] with me,* and I shall be much obliged to you if you will inform me what Day will be agreeable to you to meet M^r M^{tris} and *Miss Stone* at my house to Dinner, I shou'd be glad if it was either Thursday or Friday, whichever Day *you please* to fix, I will send to Mr Stone to let them know. I long to see you my D^r H, let me have that pleasure as soon as you can, till when and Ever I remain with the *firmest* attachment My D^r L: most faithfully and affectionately yours [etc.]' (CCLN 283)

The following day was less fraught, and Haydn seems to have quickly recovered his enthusiasm for the London life; he dined in the company of English Mozartians at Stephen Storace's together with Michael Kelly and the two *prima donnas* Nancy Storace and Gertrud Mara. As it was the eve of the king's birthday 'All the bells in London are rung from

*These five words, the only possibly incriminating phrase in the whole correspondence, were originally doubly underlined by Haydn, but later erased.

8 o'clock in the evening to 9 o'clock, and also in honour of the Queen.' (CCLN 259)

The following evening Haydn went to Vauxhall. This was the most elaborate and tempting of London's pleasure gardens and, moreover, one that was open to all classes of citizenry. Friedrich Wendeborn, an earlier German visitor to London, had also made the trip across the river, and reported on the sybaritic scene:

'The famous gardens of Vauxhall, so celebrated on the continent, and of which there are so many feeble imitations, are within the parish of Lambeth. Various classes of people resort thither in the evening during the summer, for different kinds of amusements; but, even a philosopher may spend there agreeable hours at a small expense. He may hear good music and singing; he may refresh himself in the cool of the evening; he may make observations on men and manners, retire in good time, and rise the next morning without in the least repenting the pleasures of the last evening. This, indeed, may not be the case with a great number of those who frequent those gardens, and derive from thence causes for a long repentance.' (Wendeborn I 352–3)

His compatriot, the Pastor Moritz, however, described the same scene and was more specific about the provenance of these seductive hazards:

'This orchestra is among a number of trees situated as in a little wood, and is an exceedingly handsome one. As you enter the garden, you immediately hear the sound of vocal and instrumental music. There are several female singers constantly hired here to sing in public. On each side of the orchestra are small boxes, with tables and benches, in which you sup. The walks before these, as well as in every other part of the garden, are crowded with people of all ranks . . . but what most astonished me, was the boldness of the women of the town; who, along with their pimps, often rushed in upon us by half dozens; and in the most shameless manner importuned us for wine, for themselves and their followers.' (Moritz 35)

68

VAUXHALL GARDENS

On the king's birthday, however, patriotism (or the weather) seems to have restrained the ladies of the town, for Haydn makes no mention of them:

'Over 30,000 lamps were burning, but because of the severe cold there were very few people present. The grounds and its variety are perhaps unique in the world. There are 155 little dining booths in various places, most charmingly situated, each comfortably seating 6 persons. There are very large alleys of trees, which form a wonderful roof above, and are magnificently illuminated. Tea, coffee and milk with almonds all cost nothing. The entrance fee is half a crown per person. The music is fairly good. A stone statue of Handel has been erected. On the 2nd inst. there was a masked ball, and on this evening they took in 3000 guineas.' (CCLN 262)

The statue of Handel was by the Frenchman Roubiliac. Until recently it stood in Novello's publishing house in Wardour Street, and can now be seen in the Victoria and Albert Museum. Haydn cannot have eaten at one of the little booths that he enumerates, or he would surely have made a note of such delicacies as 'frothed syllabub, fragrant tea, sliced ham, scraped beef and burnt champagne' – although the catering was so parsimonious that it was said that the ham was sliced so thin you could read your programme through it.

A day or two later Haydn was intensely moved by a more innocent experience – a response he shared with Handel and Berlioz.

'8 days before Pentecost I heard 4,000 charity children in St Paul's Church sing the song noted below. One performer indicated the tempo. No music ever moved me so deeply in my whole life as this devotional and innocent

N.B.: All the children are newly clad, and enter in procession. The organist first played the melody very nicely and simply, and then they all began to sing at once.' (CCLN 261)

Years later, remembering the incident for Dies, Haydn said: 'I stood there and wept like a child.'

During these summer months, Haydn had been receiving communications from his patron, Prince Anton, asking that he return to the service of the Esterházys. Haydn had put him off once already, but now, with the London concert season over, and his prince demanding his attendance at the Coronation of Francis II in Frankfurt, 'Yesterday I purchased a little trunk,' he writes on 13 June; 'I shall leave London at the end of the month'.

Mrs Schroeter finds it is time to return her borrowings, her affection as emphatic as ever, even though her grammar is a little disturbed at the thought of parting from her beloved:

'My D^st Inclosed I send you the verses you was so kind as to lend me, and am very much obliged to you for permitting me to take a Copy of them. pray inform me *how you do*, and let me know *my* D^t L: when you will *dine* with me. I shall be *happy to see you* to dinner either to *morrow* or *tuesday* whichever is most convenient to you, I am *truly anxious* and *impatient* to *see you*, and I wish to have as much of *your company* as possible: indeed *my* D^st H: I *feel* for *you* the *fondest* and *tenderest affection* the *human heart* is capable of, and I ever am with the *firmest* attachment my D^t Love
most Sincerely, Faithfully
and most affectionately yours [etc.]'

Haydn, however, forewent her company in favour of a trip to Ascot the following day, taking in Windsor on the way. He reports at length:

'The castle chapel at Windsor is a very old but splendid building; the high altar cost 50,000 fl. It shows the ascension of Christ in stained glass. This year, 1792, in the side altar to the right, a smaller one, showing Christ appearing to the Shepherds, was completed. This small one is valued more highly than the large one. The view from the terrace is divine.

'. . . from there 8 miles to Ascot Heath to see the races. These horse races are run on a large field, especially prepared for them, and on this field is a large circular track 2 English miles long and 6 fathoms wide. It is all very smooth and even, and the whole field has a gentle upwards slope. At the summit the circle stops curving and becomes a straight line about 2000 paces long; along this straight line, stalls of various sizes, or rather an ampitheatre, have been erected, some of which hold 2 to 3 hundred persons. The others are smaller. In the middle there is one for the Prince of Wales and high personages. The places in these stalls cost from 1 to 42 shillings per person. Opposite the Prince of Wales' stall is erected a high platform with a bell over it, on which platform stand several persons who have been specially chosen and sworn, and they give the first signal with the bell for the performers to line up in front of the platform. When they are ready, the bell is rung a second time, and at the first stroke they ride off at once. Whoever is the first to traverse the circle of 2 miles and return to the platform from which they started, receives the prize. In the first Heeth [heat] there were 3 riders, and they had to go round the circle twice without stopping. They did this double course in 5 minutes. No stranger will believe this unless they have seen it themselves. The 2nd time there were seven riders; when they were in the middle of the circle, all 7 were in the same line, but as soon as they came nearer some fell behind, but never more than about 10 paces; and just when you think that one of them is rather near the goal, and people make large bets on him at this moment, another rushes past him at very close quarters and with unbelievable force reaches the winning place. The riders are very lightly clad in silk, and each one has a different colour, so that you can recognize him more easily; no boots, a little cap on his head, they are all as lean as a greyhound and lean as their horses. Each one is weighed in, and a certain weight is allowed him, in proportion to the strength of the horse, and if the rider is too light he must put on heavier clothes, or they hang some lead on him. The horses are of the finest possible breed, light, with very thin feet, the hair of their neck tied into braids, the hoofs very delicate. As soon as they hear the sound of the bell, they dash off at once with the greatest force. Every leap of the horses is 22 feet long. These horses are very expensive. The Prince of Wales paid £8000 for one some years ago, and sold it again for £6000; but he won £50,000 with it the first time. Among other things a single large stall is erected, wherein the Englishmen place their bets. The King has his own stall at one side. I saw 5 heats on the first day, and despite a heavy rain there were 2000 vehicles, all full of people, and 3 times as many common people on foot. Besides this, there are all sorts of other things – puppet-plays, hawkers, horror plays – which go on during the races; many tents with refreshments, all kinds of wine and beer, and many Io-players (in English it is written Eo), a game which is forbidden in London. This horse racing went on 5 days in succession. I was there on the 2nd day; the beginning was at 2 o'clock and it went on till 5, the 3rd day till half-past 6, though there were but 3 Heaths, because it happened twice that 3 riders came in first together, and thus they had to race four times to decide the winner.'   (CCLN 276, 255–7)

It is a pity that Haydn so rarely mentions the company with whom he made these journeys; certainly the trip to Ascot was without Mrs Schroeter, since she left a note for him suggesting dinner, and hoping he had been 'much amused with the Race'. Whoever was guiding Haydn (can it have been the ever-thoughtful Salomon?) had the brilliant idea of making a diversion on the way home to visit William Herschel, the famous astronomer, at his home and observatory in Slough. Since Herschel had been an oboist in the Hanover Guards until leaving Germany at the age of twenty-one, there was no language barrier for Haydn:

'On 15th June I went from Windsor to [Slough] to Doctor Hershel, where I saw the great telescope. It is 40 feet long and 5 feet in diameter. The machinery is very big, but so ingenious that a single man can put it in motion with the greatest ease. There are also 2 smaller [telescopes], of which one is 22 feet long and magnifies 6000 times. The King had 2 made for himself, each of which measures 12 feet. He paid him 1000 guineas for them. In his younger days Dr Hershel was in the Prussian service as an oboe player. During the seven-years' war he deserted with his brother and went to England, where he supported himself as a musician for many years: he became an organist at Bath, but gradually turned more to astronomy. After having provided himself with the necessary instruments, he left Bath, rented a room near Windsor, and studied day and night. His landlady was a widow, fell in love with him, married him, and gave him a dowry of £100,000. Besides this he has a yearly pension for life of £500 from the King, and his wife, at the age of 45, presented him with a son this year, 1792. Ten years ago he had his sister come, and she is of the greatest assistance to him in his observations. Sometimes he sits for 5 or 6 hours under the open sky in the bitterest cold weather.'

(CCLN 254–5)

Another visitor to the house was Burney, making frequent trips to try out sections of his latest epic project, *Astronomy, an historical & didactic Poem, in XII Books*. It is probably merciful that almost nothing has survived of this enterprise, although Burney's enthusiasm for space travel 'perhaps to planets nearest the Earth such as Mars & Venus' is touching. The proposed transport is less than convincing:

'If I had wit enough, or energy of mind sufficient to be *mad* ab^t anything now, it w^d be ab^t *Balons* – I think them the most wild, Romantic, pretty playthings for grown Gentlemen that have ever been invented & that the subject, as well as the thing, lifts one to the Clouds, whenever one talks of it.' (Lonsdale 385)

Haydn, despite his day with Herschel, remained resolutely earth-bound in his travel plans. His little trunk was packed, and he had reached an agreement with Salomon to return for the 1793 season. He had also received his last endearments from Mrs Schroeter. The final social engagement seems to have been a typically English garden party, which merits a

CHARLES BURNEY
BY GEORGE DANCE

mention in the Notebook, together with a recipe which presumably derives from the same event: 'On 23rd June 1792 the Duchess of York gave a dinner for 180 persons under a large tent in her garden. I saw the same . . . The Prince of Wales' punch: 1 bottle champagne, 1 bottle Burgundy, 1 bottle rum, 10 lemons, 2 oranges, $1\frac{1}{2}$ lbs. of sugar.'*

(CCLN 270)

Suitably refreshed, Haydn quit England, and journeying via Bonn and Frankfurt was reinstated in Vienna by the end of July, ready to resume duties to his prince. But even with his exceptional modesty he must have noticed the contrast between the ecstatic welcome he had been given by the English press, and the reception on his arrival home. Not a single Viennese paper noted his return.

* Dr H. C. Robbins Landon, the doyen of Haydn scholars, fulfils every possible requirement of musicology by personally attesting to the excellence of this drink.

INTERLUDE

Haydn failed to keep his promise for the following season. Although announced with confidence by Salomon during December, the January bulletins were less certain. An unspecified but 'severe indisposition' was preventing him from undertaking the journey; Salomon had written 'very pressing letters to entreat his attendance'; in the meanwhile 'his place will be filled by Mr Clementi'.

With the opening concert only three weeks away, more elaborate excuses begin to appear: the *Morning Herald* (18 January 1793) laments that 'Poor Haydn continues in Germany very ill: but composing for England and promising to come over when he can. He is afflicted with the tedious and painful disorder, a *polypus* in the nose, for which he is immediately about to suffer an operation.'

The famous polypus, which along with his pock-marked skin gave Haydn every reason for describing himself as 'no beauty', would surely have roused some sympathy in the thwarted public; but the idea of Haydn suffering any operation for its removal was a very unlikely fiction. He had all too recently had a narrow escape from just such an attempt at the hands of John Hunter, the distinguished medical scholar and surgeon (whose wife was to provide the texts for many of Haydn's later English songs). Haydn himself recalled the event for Dies, and surely had not kept it a secret from his English acquaintances at the time.

'In London, Haydn came to know the famous surgeon H[unter], "a man", said Haydn, "who almost daily performed surgical operations and always successfully. He had inspected my polyp and offered to free me of this nuisance. I had half agreed, but the operation was put off and at last I thought no more of it. Shortly before my departure, Mr H. asked me to come and see him about some urgent matters. I went there. After the first exchange of greetings, a few brawny fellows entered the room, grabbed me and wanted to force me into a chair. I yelled, kicked and hit until I had freed myself and made clear to Mr H., who already had his instruments ready for the operation, that I did not want to undergo the operation. He was very astonished at my obstinacy, and it seemed to me that he pitied me for not wanting to undergo the happy experience of enjoying his skill. I excused myself, saying that there was not time because of my forthcoming departure, and took my leave of him." '

(Dies: Landon 178)

In fact, Haydn himself seems to have offered no excuse for his absence. We may speculate that he was tired, happy to be in German-speaking lands again, unwilling to risk a return to the exacting routine of London concert life without a sufficient supply of new compositions to hand. He had discovered to his – and Mrs Schroeter's – distress that the strain of combining a full social life with composition in London was beginning to tell. He was now sixty and nobody's slave.

The political turmoil in Europe, however, must have been one of the strongest deterrents to travel in 1793, and the imminence of war soon distracted the British from any abnormalities in their concert calendars. Even Parson Woodforde, in the security of his Norfolk living, was moved from his parochial gossip to include international problems alongside the diurnal feastings: 'Counter-Revolution in France, the King, Queen and Dauphin have made their escape. Dinner to day Hash-Mutton and a Suet Pudding &c.'

And, later . . . 'Dinner to day Souse, Veal Pye and Calfs Heart rosted. Billy Bidewells People brought our Newspapers from Norwich. The King of France Louis 16 inhumanly and unjustly beheaded on Monday last by his cruel, bloodthirsty Subjects. Dreadful times I am afraid are approaching to all Europe.'

'Is this the end of the 18th Centy, so enlightened & so philosophical?' cried Burney with real emotion. 'I can neither think, talk, or write abt anything else than the abominations of France'. The 'Lottery of Holy Guillotine' – itself the invention of a harpsichord-maker – had begun.

In the face of the Terror, or, more accurately, the Declaration of the Rights of Man (and the English advocacy of the same progressive ideals by Tom Paine, a friend of Michael Kelly), even the small group of Haydn's English friends were variously aligned. Stephen Storace had composed a 'Lamentation of Marie Antoinette, late Queen of France, on the Morning of her Execution' that confirmed his Royalist affiliations, and Mrs Papendiek had already noted the military preparations both in London and the provinces.

'In almost every town and borough societies were formed, against Government authority, of different ranks and classes of people. In London some of these meetings were called "The Debating Societies", "The Corresponding Societies", "Nights of the People", &c . . . The militia was embodied, attendance was required for practice a given number of days in each month, and they were kept in constant military order so as to be also ready at call if required.'

(Papendiek II 290–2)

Burney himself was adamantly for the existing social structure, and despised 'the Mob'.

'To shake hands wth sweep-chimneys, Coal-heavers, churls, clodpolls, soldiers, & sailors, & assure them that they are our *true sovereigns*, have a right to our possessions without work or service, & that without education, cultivation of talents, or intellect, they are equal & even superior to those who have usually been thought men of learning, abilities, and genius. These are the reforms intended . . . As to the *majesty of the people*, I own myself a determined rebel to all *tyrants*, but to none so much as to that monster. If we were really oppressed, old as I am, & crippled by Rheumatism, I w^{d} endeavour to pull a trigger against the oppressors, if fair means w^{d} not do.'

(Lonsdale 364)

In the provinces it was less easy to be extreme without igniting antagonisms, and in Leicester William Gardiner solved the problem most diplomatically by declaring that

'France and England were as different as wax and tallow' – but declined to say which was the wax and which was the tallow.

The 'democratic' left-wingers were understandably less public in their pronouncements, particularly when politics was not their business. Michael Kelly had made the trip to Paris, he claimed, purely 'to see what I could pick up by way of dramatic novelty for Drury Lane'. William Shield, on holiday in the Savoy Alps, was so determinedly egalitarian that he wrote from the Mont Cenis pass to the revolutionary poet Thomas Holcroft:

'I thought it degraded the race of men too much to suffer them to carry me in a sedan over this immense mountain: in consequence of which we had mules; and after riding about one mile, reflection told me that I was shortening the life of the animal . . . and as I saw women walking I was resolved to do the same.' (Holcroft III 297)

Both Holcroft and Shield were good friends of Haydn (Shield a fellow freemason as well), yet they can hardly have seen eye-to-eye with Storace. Lord Abingdon and Charles Burney were two of Haydn's staunchest supporters – the one a 'progressive', the other a die-hard Royalist . . . one wonders whether English musical life was impervious to divisions of political thought, despite the declaration of war (yet again) with France. Or did each individual in Haydn's circle share in Dr Burney's dream?

'I sh^d think I did the world a signal piece of service, if, one night or other, when its inhabitants were all fast asleep, I could, by the wave of a magic wand, wipe away every idea of that kind, smack smooth, out of their brains, or send them down forever to the bottom of their *dimenticatos*; & in their room, pour into their precious noddles, with a large funnel, the love of Music, poetry, & the fine arts, or other good-humoured, amusing, & improving pursuits, ingenious or scientific, as they please. Let them study mathematics, optics, metaphysics, & all the *ics* & *tics* in the world, except *Politics*. How good-humoured & happy they w^d all come down to breakfast, the next morning!' (Lonsdale 370)

79

HAYDN'S SECOND VISIT

Much to Burney's delight, love of music was gratified above politics in 1794, when, despite the coldest winter in living memory, and a disastrous British retreat in Holland, Haydn decided to fulfil what he had promised for the previous year. With the reluctant permission of his prince, on 19 January he once more took to the road across war-swept Europe, this time with his assistant and copyist Johann Elssler as travelling companion (who, sadly, seems to have left us no 'beneath-stairs' account of foreign life). He travelled in relative comfort in a private coach loaned to him by that great patron Baron van Swieten. His trunk was packed with new pieces commissioned for England – piano trios, a set of six string quartets,* and fresh orchestral works for Salomon. Although no harm befell him from the Napoleonic turmoil, Dies tells us of one incident involving the military in Wiesbaden which he must have had from Haydn himself.

'In the inn where Haydn was staying, he heard someone next door to his room playing the favourite Andante with the drum beat† on the pianoforte. He counted on the player being his friend and politely entered the room from which the music was coming. There he found several Prussian officers, who were all great admirers of his music, and when he finally said who he was, wouldn't take him at his word, that he was Haydn. "Impossible! Impossible! You Haydn? – A man of such advanced years! – How does that correspond with the fire in your music? – No, we'll never believe it." They went on in this tone so long, and continued doubting, till Haydn showed them a letter from their king, which he luckily happened to have in his luggage. Now the officers

---

* Nowadays confusingly divided into two groups of three quartets, and known as Opus 71 and Opus 74.
† The 'Surprise' Symphony.

showered him with affection and he had to remain in their company until well after midnight. Haydn was sorry to leave his newly-won friends; he departed and arrived in London as early as 4 February 1794.'　　　　　　　　(Dies: Landon 231)

'As early as' seems an odd remark from Dies, since the journey took a couple of days longer than it had in 1790, and Haydn was hardly punctual for Salomon's series, which had been advertised as opening on the 3rd. Since the public had been assured that 'Dr Haydn will supply the Concerts with new Compositions, and direct the Execution of them at the Piano Forte', the opening was postponed to 'Monday se'nnight', pending the arrival of composer and trunk.

Haydn must have been doubly pleased to find on his arrival not only that competition from the Professional Concert had ceased, but that Salomon's other attractions would include the bass singer who had created the part of Osmin in Mozart's *Seraglio*, and one of Europe's finest violinists, now a refugee from the Terrors in France.

CONCERTS, SINGERS, &c.

'The Professional is dropt, – in consequence SALOMON's will be entirely unopposed until after Easter, when the promised Concert at the Opera House is to be given.

'Thus the HANOVER SQUARE will have had *ten* nights performance completely unrivalled. HAYDN is to be at the Piano Forte, and every nerve is to be exerted to leave an impression deeper than ever of this excellent band.

'FISCHER is an admirable Singer – His voice is more *even* than DAVID's; it is a bass running up into a tenor without *falsetto* – it is expected, he will be more to the English taste, than any singer they have ever heard.

'VIOTTI has been selecting some fine thoughts for *Concerto playing*, which for sublimity and simplicity is unequalled – *Duetti*, so much admired between SALOMON and himself, will be of course pursued. . . .'　　　　　　　(*Oracle* 25.i.94)

As it turned out, Fischer was even more delayed than Haydn had been, and his enormous range (from lowest D to top A – 'all round, even and in tune') was not heard until a later concert.

Sufficient novelty, however, was provided by a new symphony [No. 99 in E flat] in which Haydn employed, for the first time, that latest orchestral invention, the clarinet. The press, sensing that another season of superlatives lay ahead, began strategically in bottom gear:

SALOMON'S CONCERT. OPENING NIGHT.
'We must of necessity be brief. And after all it may be best, when the *chef d'oeuvre* of the great HAYDN is the subject.
' "Come then, expressive SILENCE, muse his praise." '
(*Oracle* 11.ii.94)

The second concert of the series, although troubled by 'Madama Mara being taken ill with a violent cold and hoarseness', contained one of Haydn's new string quartets, which 'gave pleasure by its variety, gaiety, and the fascination of its melody and harmony'. Quartet playing in public concerts, rather than the normal domestic or court surroundings, was something new for Haydn. The experience of hearing his earlier chamber works played by Salomon's quartet during his first visit generated in this set of quartets a new type of public chamber music. They were designed to make their effects before a large audience, sharing a programme with symphonies and concertos, and capitalizing on the professional virtuosity of Salomon as his leader. Although the quartets were actually dedicated to Count Apponyi, a fellow freemason of Haydn's in Vienna, it is clear that they were written with Salomon's performances in mind.

For the first time we find introductions added to the first movements of these quartets – the sudden loud chords, it has been suggested, were Haydn's method of silencing a large and talkative audience; there are more 'popular' melodies (especially in the finales); and the minuets are outspokenly concert pieces. Nevertheless, Haydn never once relinquished the quartet ideal of democratic discourse between four equals – a truly amazing reconciliation of the private and public philosophies.

Although the press noted the unexpected technical demands of these works ('so difficult . . . as to require all the powers of Crosdill of the rapid bow'), William Gardiner, whom we left observing Haydn through his telescope at the Handel Commemoration, still saw these works as conversation-pieces.

'An intelligent lady said, that when she heard a quartett of Haydn's, she fancied herself present at the conversation of four agreeable persons. She thought the first violin had the air of an eloquent man of genius, of middle age, who supported a conversation, the subject of which he had suggested. In the second violin, she recognised a friend of the first, who sought by all possible means to display him to advantage, seldom thought of himself, and kept up the conversation rather by assenting to what was said by others, than by advancing any ideas of his own. The alto was a grave, learned, and sententious man. He supported the discourse of the first violin by laconic maxims, striking for their truth. The bass was a worthy old lady, rather inclined to chatter, who said nothing of much consequence, and yet was always desiring to put in a word. But she gave an additional grace to the conversation, and while she was talking, the other interlocutors had time to breathe. It was, however, evident, that she had a secret inclination for the alto, which she preferred to the other instruments.'

(Bombet: Gardiner 63–4)

Gardiner's passion for Haydn's quartets eventually induced him to add religious words to selected movements, which were then published as vocal music under the title of 'Sacred Melodies'; Haydn's views on this adaptation are not recorded. On the other hand, Gardiner quotes as evidence of the need to fulfil a composer's exact intentions the fact that 'Haydn sent for the three Moralts [members of a famous string quartet] from Vienna, to show the Londoners the time in which the minuets in his quartettes should be played. He considered they were spoilt by being hurried, nor could he dispossess them of the idea that quickness was the essential character of the moderns.' (Gardiner 266–7)

Mr Fischer, 'the vocal novelty from Berlin', made the hoped-for impact at his eventual appearance in the third concert: 'His first Song was vehemently encored, and he narrowly escaped the fatigue of repeating the second.' Thereafter the series proceeded on its expected course, with a welcome for Madame Mara recovered and in good form (though accused by the *Morning Chronicle* of repeating the same songs too frequently), continued wonder at the voice of Mr Fischer ('astonishing both in body and compass'), a raised eyebrow at the ephemeral, and occasionally inaudible, glass harmonica, a murmur of sympathy for the incidental hazard ('Madame Delaval's harp was most cruelly strung. She broke three strings – however, her finger was brilliant'). There were, of course, universal encores for Haydn's music – 'For *Grace* and *Science*, what is like it?'

The greatest single success of all Haydn's London compositions was yet to come. The 'Surprise' Symphony had, up to now, topped the bill; however, in the eighth concert appeared what we know as Symphony No. 100, but what was usually referred to at that time as the 'Grand Overture with the Militaire Movement'. Mara, Fischer, the glass harmonica, all were forgotten in the uproar that greeted a work which so invigoratingly captured the mood of the time, with the outburst of cymbals, triangle and bass drum (the 'Turkish music') in the slow movement.

'Encore! encore! encore! resounded from every seat: the Ladies themselves could not forbear. It is the advancing to battle; and the march of men, the sounding of the charge, the thundering of the onset, the clash of arms, the groans of the wounded, and what may well be called the hellish roar of war increase to a climax of horrid sublimity! which, if others can conceive, he alone can execute; at least he alone hitherto has effected these wonders.' (*Morning Chronicle* 9.iv.94)

For Haydn's own Benefit Concert, which followed on 2 May, the symphony was repeated 'By Desire', coupled with the attractions of Viotti, Mr Fischer and Dussek, whose originality had been gradually appreciated during this season ('the first movement abounded in the usual mad flights of the master'). 'Tickets, at 10s 6d each', we read, 'to be had of Dr Haydn, No.1, Bury-street, St James.' This change of address explains why we find no correspondence from Rebecca Schroeter during this period: from Bury Street to Buckingham Gate was but a short constitutional along the Mall, and clearly communication was verbal, and more frequent. Haydn's Notebooks, however, still supply us with a vivacious assortment of vignettes, including the musician's evidence of the rowdiness that he was escaping by leaving Great Pulteney Street.

da Capo

'A gang of rowdy fellows sang this song with all their might. They yelled so loudly that you could hear them 1000 paces away from the street, in every nook and cranny.' (CCLN 278)

It is about this time, in the summer of 1794, that Haydn began to note in great detail facts and figures about the British Navy and its admirals, topics of conversation that must have been uppermost in many Londoners' minds. The war with France was not prospering, and as the fleet set sail down the Channel on 2 May, escorting the British merchant convoys bound for America, a naval encounter with French forces seemed imminent. Eyes turned to Admiral Lord Howe, the grand old man of the sea, at sixty-eight still 'undaunted as a rock and as silent'; but could even he overcome the natural hazards of a Georgian administration?

'A very good English toast, or drink-your-health: the first 2 words of the 3rd Psalm. "Lord! How" *etc* [are they increased that trouble me!], that is, Lord Howe, the great English soldier.' (CCLN 300)

'Milord Chatam, President of the War Office and brother of Minister Pitt, was so drunk for 3 days that he couldn't even sign his name, and thus occasioned that Lord Howe couldn't leave London, and together with the whole fleet couldn't sail away.'* (CCLN 298)

* This picture of Chatham is reinforced by Farington's report that 'an intimate friend of Ld. Chatham had spoken to him on the inconvenience attending his laying in bed till the day is advanced, as Officers & c were kept waiting. Ld. Chatham said it did not signify it was an indulgence He cd. not give up.'

Such is war. Eventually, after many days of searching the blank Atlantic for the French fleet, Lord Howe engaged with the enemy off Ushant. Frustration rose when two days of fog kept the two fleets within earshot, but out of sight of each other. Sunday 1 June dawned clear and sunny, and with the enormous ships at such close quarters, sometimes with two ships so jammed together that the gun-ports could not be opened and the gunners had to fire through them, the encounter was one of intimate slaughter rather than strategy. The end of the day announced a British victory, and Lord Howe was carried from the quarter-deck, too exhausted to stand any longer. His prizes were seven of the French battleships, now limping and demasted, and one so badly holed that it sank before reaching port. Midshipman Parker (aged 11) wrote home in jubilation: 'We have conquered the rascals.'*

News of 'The Glorious First of June' took ten days to reach London. When it did, the illuminations, street celebrations and breaking of windows went on for three days.

'On 11th June the whole city was illuminated because of the capture of 7 French warships; a great many windows were broken. On the 12th and 13th the whole city was illuminated again. The common people behaved very violently on this occasion. In every street they shot off not only small but also large guns, and this went on the whole night.'   (CCLN 287)

The London theatres responded with remarkable alacrity to the festive mood. 'At the King's Theatre', Parke remembers, 'a grand performance was given on the 2d of July, in celebration of the glorious victory obtained by Earl Howe of the fleet of the French republic. The performance consisted of the comic opera, "Le Serva padrona" [by Giovanni Paisiello], with appropriate ballets; after which Madame Banti, who had become extremely popular, sang our national song "Rule Britannia", in which she was vociferously encoured,

* The engagement is graphically described in Farington's Diary for 18 July.

86

although her bad English amounted almost to burlesque! This clearly shows that fashion, like love, is blind.'

(Parke I 190)

Sheridan, at Drury Lane, was not content with a mere repeat; he insisted on a new and spectacular 'musical entertainment' which, against all the predictions of the theatre's employees, was completed in those three days. Many hands contributed to both libretto and music (including Storace, Linley and Kelly), but the *pièce de résistance* was a sea-fight between two model fleets, which slid in from opposite wings and engaged in gun-fire: patriotically 'the spectators coughed and enjoyed the powder'. On the first night alone more than £1000 was taken, and both cast and audience concluded the evening by singing 'Rule, Britannia'. However, the initial enthusiasm for this confection must have died down by July, when Farington found neither it, nor the theatre, to his taste.

'The first of June is heavy & ill suited I think to work on the people properly, it dwells too much on the consequences of war.

'Drury Lane Theatre is an instance of the worst taste I ever saw in a large building, – disproportioned in design and frippery in the execution.'   (Farington I 211)

In the meantime, Haydn, exhausted by the London season but attracted by the idea of seeing the ruined French ships that were now on display at Spithead, decided to make a trip *incognito* to visit Portsmouth, and accepted an invitation from the Governor of the Isle of Wight, Thomas Orde. Making an early departure from London on 9 July (the Portsmouth stage left at 5 a.m.), Haydn took in Hampton Court on the way, admiring the huge paintings by Verrio over the King's Staircase, and finding the gardens similar to those he knew at Esterháza. He arrived in Portsmouth at eight in the evening, and the next day saw the shattered remains of the French ships.

'I went aboard the French ship-of-the-line called *le just*; it has 80 cannon; the English, or rather Lord Howe, captured it. The 18 cannon in the harbour-fortress are 36-pounders. The ship is terribly shot to pieces. The great mast, which is 10 feet 5 inches in circumference, was cut off at the very bottom and lay stretched on the ground. A single cannon-ball, which passed through the captain's room, killed 14 sailors . . .

'The Dockyard, or the place where ships are built, is of an enormous size, and has a great many splendid buildings. But I couldn't go there, because I was a foreigner. Hard by is a new and most splendid ship-of-the-line with 110 cannon, called the *Prince of Wales*. The King and his family stayed 3 days in the Dockyard at the *gouverneur's* house.'   (CCLN 292)

It is hard to imagine Haydn as a security risk, although from the series of nautical jottings that follow in his Notebook it seems he must have spent much time (with his broken English?) interrogating naval personnel, and even making small sketches when words failed.

'Ebb-tide and flood-tide every 7 hours. In Spring the tide recedes 14 feet, during the rest of the season only 7 feet.'

'Every ship-of-the-line, or man-of-war, has 3 masts, like-wise a Frigate.

'Most of them have 3 decks.

'A Brig has 2 masts.

'A Cutter has only 1 mast.

'Every ship-of-the-line must have at least 64 cannon.

'A Cutter has but 14, at the most 16 cannon.

'A fire-ship has 2 masts. In the middle of its sails it has 2 large and long cross-beams with round, pointed double irons:

'When they come near an enemy ship, this iron grapples the rigging or even the sails, whereupon one sets the ship on fire, so that the other ship which is grappled to it has to burn, too. The crew saves itself in the little lifeboats which they take with them . . .

'A Cockswan is a kind of subaltern who, when his Capitain goes to sea, stands at attention next to him. A capitain generally has his special crew, all identically dressed, which he takes with him to his port. At 12 o'clock I was in the neighbourhood of the fleet when the 12 o'clock bells were rung.

'It is said that Juli[u]s Caesar, having had to flee, landed quite by accident on this island, and is supposed to have said: this is the port of the Gods. Godsport. There are 1500 patients in this hospital, among them 300 sailors who were with Lord Howe in the last naval battle.' (CCLN 291)

Haydn's humanitarian feelings would surely have been shocked to know that at this very time the artist Rowlandson was exploiting the aftermath of the battle not by viewing battered ships, but in the hospital observing the sick-bed of a dying French officer making his will. Henry Angelo, his companion, was more sensitive: 'His comrades were standing by, consoling him, some grasping his hand, shedding tears. This scene was too much for me, and made such an impression on my mind that I hastened away; but I could not persuade Rowlandson to follow me, his inclination to make a sketch of the dying moment getting the better of his feelings.'   (Angelo II 293)

We might wish that Rowlandson had remained outside, and devoted his attentions to Haydn. Instead, Haydn reports, 'I met Lauterburg, the famous painter' – Loutherbourg (in more conventional orthography) was presumably collecting material for the great battle painting that now hangs in the National Maritime Museum.

From Portsmouth Haydn crossed to 'Reid . . . Reed . . . *Ryde*' (he finally got the spelling right) on 'L'Isle of Whight'. His first observation was that the island was 64 miles in circumference, his next that 'Newport is a nice little town; the people look just like the Germans and mostly have black hair', and, very soon, 'I left Cowes at 4 o'clock in the afternoon for Southampton, where I spent the night. It is a little town on a peninsular'. Clearly Mr Orde, despite having a house which 'commands the most magnificent view over the ocean', was himself unnoteworthy; 'a cold, cautious, slow and sententious man, tolerably well informed, with a mind neither powerful nor feeble'* hardly seems the ideal host for Haydn. However, as consolation, there was 'On the way back a good dinner at Farnham'.

Back in London, Haydn was witness to another massacre, this time musical:

'SPECTAS, ET TU SPECTABERE is the inscription over the curtain in the Little Haymarket Theatre. I was there on 29th July 1794: they gave a National opera, N.B. a piece in Scottish costumes. The men were dressed in flesh-coloured breeches, with white and red ribbons twisted round their stockings, a short, brightly-coloured, striped masons' apron [i.e. kilt], brown coat and waistcoat, over the coat a large, broad ensign's sash in the same style as the apron, and black

* Sir Jonah Barrington, in 'The Decline and Fall of the Irish Nation'.

cap shaped like a shoe and trimmed with ribbons. The women all in white muslin, brightly coloured ribbons in their hair, very broad bands in the same style round their bodies, also for their hats. They perform the same abominable trash as at Sadlers Wells. A fellow yelled an aria so horribly and with such exaggerated grimaces that I began to sweat all over. N.B. He had to repeat the aria. *O che bestie!*'

(CCLN 294–5)

What Haydn refrained from mentioning was that, for the 'Shipwreck' music in Act II of *Auld Robin Gray*, the 'composer', Samuel Arnold, had simply lifted the 'Earthquake' movement from Haydn's *Seven Last Words*. One can imagine how blisteringly Dr Burney would have treated such sacrilege, though Haydn may have been less protective. 'The Earthquake Finale' had, after all, been called on to conclude both his own and Salomon's Benefits in the first season.

On 2 August Haydn made his longest English journey, this time bound for Bath, where he was to stay with the famous *castrato* singer Rauzzini (the man for whom Mozart had written 'Exsultate, Jubilate').

THE GLORIOUS FIRST OF JUNE BY LOUTHERBOURG

'It's 107 miles from London. The Mail Coach does this distance in 12 hours. I lived at the house of Herr Rauzzini, a *Musicus* who is very famous, and who in his time was one of the greatest singers. He has lived there 19 years, supports himself by the Subscription Concerts which are given in the Winter, and by giving lessons. He is a very nice and hospitable man. His summer house, where I stayed, is situated on a rise in the middle of a most beautiful neighbourhood, from which you can see the whole city. Bath is one of the most beautiful cities in Europe. All the houses are built of stone; this stone comes from quarries in the surrounding mountains; it is very soft, so soft, in fact, that it's no trouble to cut it up into any desired shape; it is very white, and the older it is, once it has been taken from the quarry, the harder it gets. The whole city lies on a slope, and that is why there are very few carriages; instead of them, there are a lot of sedan-chairs, who will take you quite a way for 6 pence. But too bad that there are so few straight roads; there are a lot of beautiful squares, on which stand the most magnificent houses, but which cannot be reached by any vehicle: they are now building a brand new and broad street.

'N.B. Today, on the 3rd, I looked at the city, and found, half-way up the hill, a building shaped like a half-moon, and more magnificent than any I had seen in London. The curve extends for 100 fathoms, and there is a Corinthian column at each fathom. The building has 3 floors. Round about it, the pavement in front of the houses is 10 feet broad for the pedestrians, and the street as wide *a proportione*; it is surrounded by an iron fence, and a terrace slopes down 50 fathoms in successive stages, through a beautiful expanse of green; on both sides there are little paths, by which one can descend very comfortably.

'Every Monday and Friday evening all the bells are rung, but apart from this, you don't hear many bells being rung. The city is not thickly populated, and in Summer one sees very few people; for the people taking the baths don't come till the beginning of October, and stay through half of February. But then a great many people come, so that in the year 1791, 25,000 persons were there. All the inhabitants live off

THE COMFORTS OF BATH BY ROWLANDSON

THE ROYAL CRESCENT AT BATH BY THOMAS MALTON

this influx, without which the city would be very poor: there are very few merchants and almost no trade, and everything is very dear. The baths are by nature very warm; one bathes in the water, and one also drinks it – generally the latter. And one pays very little: to bathe it costs 3 shillings at all times. I made the acquaintance there of Miss Brown, a charming person of the best *conduit*; a good pianoforte player, her mother a most beautiful woman. The city is now building a most splendid room for guests taking the cure.'

(CCLN 295–6)

Dr Harington, another Bath acquaintance, produced a poetic compliment to Haydn:

> *What Art expresses and what Science praises*
> *Haydn the Theme of both to Heaven raises.*

The composer reciprocated by setting the words to music, doubtless noting their superiority to many of the other effusions that were directed at him by adulatory Bathonians. Only one poem appears to have been touched by the Muse during all Haydn's time in England, and this came from the pen of Thomas Holcroft. For once, expurgation is unnecessary.

TO HAYDN

> *Who is the mighty master, that can trace*
> *Th'eternal lineaments of Nature's face?*
> *'Mid endless dissonance, what mortal ear*
> *Could e'er her peal of perfect concord hear?*
> *Answer, Oh, HAYDN! strike the magic chord!*
> *And as thou strik'st, reply, and proof afford.*
>
> *Whene'er thy Genius, flashing native fire,*
> *Bids the soul tremble with the trembling lyre,*
> *The hunter's clatt'ring hoof, the peasant-shout,*
> *The warrior on-set, or the battle's rout,*
> *Din, clamour, uproar, murder's midnight knell,*
> *Hyaena shrieks, the warhoop scream and yell –*
> *All sounds, however mingled, strange, uncouth,*
> *Resolve to fitness, system, sense and truth!*

To others noise and jangle; but to thee
'Tis one grand solemn swell of endless harmony.

When dark and unknown terrors intervene,
And men aghast survey the horrid scene,
Then, when rejoicing fiends flit, gleam and scowl,
And bid the huge tormented tempest howl;
When fire-fraught thunders roll, and whirlwinds rise,
And earthquakes bellow to the frantic skies,
'Till the distracted ear, in racking gloom,
Suspects the wreck of worlds, and gen'ral doom;
Then HAYDN stands, collecting Nature's tears,
And consonance sublime amid confusion hears.
                                        (*Morning Chronicle* 12.ix.94)

With the *Sun* reassuring its readers that Haydn 'is now tolerably acquainted with our language', we might hope that he could appreciate the poem without translation, although his own correspondence with Holcroft in English makes this seem unlikely.

'Dear Sir!

I tack me the liberty to Send you the Canon, and the 2 Songs and if is possible, I self will come to you to day, o to morrow. I was oblieged to tack a Medicine to Day, perhaps I see you this Evening.

I am

       Sir with the greatest Respect
           Your
           Oblig Ser[v]
               Haydn' (CCLN 144–5)

Holcroft was translating Haydn's songs (why did Haydn have to write to him in English?), and although Farington thought him 'a disagreeable companion, being addicted to dispute on all subjects', he numbered amongst his close friends William Hazlitt and Charles Lamb, as well as Salomon and Haydn. The latter's music he would vehemently defend, even in the face of Mozart's compositions; Mozart was 'undoubtably a man of uncommon genius, but not a

Haydn'. And, after one evening's music-making, Holcroft noted:

'Music at Mr Mackenzie's. Haydn's symphony quintetto and Mozart: both men of uncommon genius, but the latter impatient after novelty and superior excellence, often forgets the flow of passion in laboriously hunting after new thoughts which, when thus introduced, have the same effect in music, as the *concetti* of the Italians have in poetry; and for these Mozart is frequently extolled as superior to Haydn.'

(Holcroft III 61)

The 'symphony quintetto' is one reminder of the fact that Haydn's works were familiar in England not only in their orchestral form, but, since concerts were rare and expensive, more frequently from the amazingly resourceful arrangements that were made by Salomon himself. All the 'London' symphonies he issued in versions scored for string quartet, flute and (optional) piano; they differ in many small details from the original Haydn text, but may very well represent changes that were made by Salomon during rehearsals. These versions lasted: Samuel Wesley could still recommend them in 1826 when lecturing in London:

'. . . certain invaluable works originally constructed for a full Band have been very ingeniously contracted for the convenient Accommodation of small musical Parties; – and among them let me instance twelve delectable Symphonies of Haydn which have been reduced from the score with extraordinary ingenuity and accurate judgement, by the late accomplished and energetic Master of his Art, John Peter Salomon, and nicely adapted for two violins, tenor, bass, flute, and a supporting accompaniment on the piano forte.'

(Wesley: *Lectures*, f.225)

Their sheer professionalism and accessibility should recommend them to performers now as then, were it not for a modern abhorrence of arrangements.

With the concert season now over, Haydn turned to composing social music on a domestic scale. It is from this eloquent and finely-wrought repertoire that we can sense the attractiveness of Haydn in private, since these intimate chamber works reflect his own circle of friends.

There is the flute-playing Lord Abingdon, whose hopes of persuading Haydn to England in the 1780s had been unfulfilled. He was consoled by frequent meetings with the composer, and eventually by a number of delightful movements for drawing-room consumption, scored for two flutes and 'cello (now known as the 'London' trios). He even collaborated with Haydn in the publication of *Twelve Sentimental Catches and Glees*; His Lordship wrote the tunes, Haydn supplied the accompaniments. Below one song text, Haydn notes: 'N.B. Lord Avington set it to music, but miserably; I did it a bit better.' (CCLN 299)

Repartee, however, seems to have been His Lordship's *forte*.

'Lord Avington had an organ built in the church on his estate. When the Archbishop of the diocese heard about it, he wrote a letter reproving him for having done this without his knowledge, inasmuch as one cannot do such a thing without previously informing the authorities. He got an answer: "The Lord gave it, and the Lord can take it away again." This is most ambiguous, but very good.'

(CCLN 300–1)

Mrs Anne Hunter, widow of the surgeon who attempted the operation on the famous polypus, lives on as the poetess of *Six Original Canzonettas, with an Accompaniment for the Piano Forte*; 'My mother bids me bind my hair' (*A Pastoral Song*, as Haydn called it) is still the most frequently heard of all his solo vocal works. 'The English words', enthused William Gardiner, 'are so appropriately adapted to the right sounds, that a native could not have executed it better'.

Anne Hunter's poetry had more to recommend it to Haydn than simply being the product of a good-looking widow. The extremes of the English drawing-room ballad were reserved for the next century; Mrs Hunter's innocent exploitation of the pastoral idiom, the naïve village maid and the love-sick swain achieved sentiment without sentimentality. Mrs Hunter's literary encouragement soon produced a second set of *Canzonettas* from Haydn; for these she not only perceptively threw in a nautical song, but adapted Metastasio and Shakespeare to her needs. But her final text for this second set does seem to have created a certain (possibly unwitting) embarrassment, which its original title 'Transport of Pleasure' made all the more explicit:

> *What though no high descent I claim,*
> *No line of Kings or race divine;*
> *Not all the mighty Sons of fame*
> *Can vaunt of joys surpassing mine . . .*
> *For mine are blooming Julia's charms,*
> *While Love my throbbing heart alarms,*
> *Transported with pleasure, I'm blest beyond measure,*
> *And die with delight in her arms.*

Haydn himself used to sing a German version of this song (in the most exalted company, as we shall shortly see), but prudence, or prudery, devised a milk-and-water text for later editions of the *Canzonettas*, plus the reassuring title of 'Content'.

Just as his friendship with Anne Hunter produced the two exquisite sets of *English Canzonettas*, so his affair with the 'lovely and aimiable' Mistress Schroeter gave birth to three of the most popular of his piano trios – or, as they were more aptly titled in those days, *Sonatas with an accompaniment for a Violin and Violoncello*. During the late years of the eighteenth century, the piano trio was an especially English form. Encouraged by pianists, publishers, and the new powerful form of piano being built by Broadwood, Haydn produced a sequence of late masterpieces for this neglected combination. One can visualize the enthusiasm in Buckingham Gate as the dedicatee of the new set of trios reached the final 'Rondo, in the Gypsies' stile'. Not even the incompatibility of modern concert instruments has managed to dampen the *joie de vivre* of that Hungarian extravaganza.

Other piano works, including the three final sonatas for piano solo, were inspired by a young virtuoso pupil of Clementi, Therese Jansen, who married the son of the engraver Bartolozzi in 1795.* Haydn was a witness to the

---

* Their daughter became the famous dancer Madame Vestris.

ceremony in St James's, Piccadilly, and his signature can still be seen in the parish register. Dies tells us of the manner in which Haydn, with Therese Jansen as an unwitting accomplice, played a trick on a German amateur violinist,

'who had acquired a skill on the violin that bordered on virtuosity, but had the bad habit of forever playing the highest notes close to the bridge. Haydn decided to make an experiment, in which he would try to see if it were not possible to cure the dilettante of his habit and give him a feeling for a solid way of playing.

'The dilettante often visited a Demoiselle J[ansen], who played the pianoforte with great dexterity, which he generally accompanied. Haydn in all secrecy wrote a Sonata for the pianoforte with the accompaniment of a violin, entitling the Sonata "Jacob's Dream", sealed it, without signing his name, and saw it reached Demoiselle J—— by a safe hand; and she did not wait to try what seemed to be an easy sonata, together with the dilettante. What Haydn had prophesied came to pass. The dilettante got stuck in the highest notes, where there was much passage work; and as soon as Demoiselle J—— was able to follow the idea of the unknown composer, who saw Jacob in his dream, and how the dilettante on this ladder soon made heavy going of it, was uncertain, tripped, stumbled and fell, she thought the situation so amusing that she could not resist laughing; while the dilettante cursed the unknown composer and boldly entertained the opinion that he couldn't write for the violin.

'It was not for five or six months that it became known that Haydn was the composer of the Sonata, and then he received a present for it from Demoiselle.'

(Dies: Landon 309–10)

Haydn's professional skills seem more closely linked to his private affections at this period of his life than almost any other, although he pronounced himself mystified why so many pretty women should have been attracted to him. 'It can hardly have been my good looks that drew them on', he later told Dies. When Dies suggested that he did have

99

something *sympathique* about him, Haydn admitted: 'They can see in me that I mean well towards everybody.'

Dies: 'That must have placed you open to many an advance.'

Haydn: 'Oh, many! but I was clever.'   (Dies: Landon 88)

Not only was Haydn clever in his relationships, but he was also too astute to commit himself in writing about his attachments – or, if he did, the evidence has had the discretion to disappear. Only in occasional jottings in the Notebooks do we catch an aside, a wistful or reassuring reflection; but even these have the ring of the proverb about them, some noted in Latin, some in German, some in Italian. 'Do not desire too great happiness or too beautiful a wife: Heaven might, in anger, grant your wish!' – 'My friend, you think I love you! In truth, you are not mistaken.'

(CCLN 267)

Haydn's relations with his own wife were discordant in the extreme; she is referred to as a Xantippe and even, on one particularly provoking occasion, as a *bestia infernale* (the most outspoken criticism he is ever found to make), which adds a passing note of melancholy to the simple adage:

> God in one's heart, a good wife on one's arm,
> The one brings salvation, the second is – warm.

(CCLN 268)

Whatever one chooses to read between the lines of the correspondence from Mrs Schroeter, there is no doubt that Haydn had an acute eye for feminine beauty. 'The most beautiful woman I ever saw' he notes – twice, and, unfortunately, about two different women. One was the poetess and musician Ann Hodges – 'a great piano player'. Haydn took back with him to Vienna one of her song settings, 'When from thy sight I waste the tedious day'; another sad little composition, with a text taken from Dryden's translation of Virgil's Second Eclogue, is preserved in Vienna in Haydn's own hand. It is, however, so uncharacteristic of him that we may imagine it also to be the work of Ann Hodges, copied as a sentimental souvenir (or possibly a salutary admonition):

THE LADIES LOOKING GLASS.
Trust not too much to that Enchanting Face
Bea[u]ty's a charm, but soon that charm will pass.

(CCLN 303)

The other 'most beautiful woman' was the wife of Tom Shaw, the politician, but the occasion was one that Haydn remembered all his life with embarrassment.

'On 14th Dec. I dined for the first time at Mr Shaw's. He received me downstairs at the door, and then led me to his wife, who was surrounded by her 2 daughters and other ladies. As I was bowing round the circle, all at once I became aware of the fact that not only the lady of the house but also her daughters and the other women each wore on the head-dress *a parte* over the front a most charming curved pearl-coloured band of 3 fingers' breadth, with the name Haydn embroidered therein in gold; and Mr Shaw wore this name on his coat, worked into the very ends of both his collars in the finest steel beads. The coat was made of the finest cloth, and with elegant steel buttons. The Mis^tris is the most beauti-ful woman I ever saw. N.B.: Her husband wanted a souvenir from me, and I gave him a tobacco-box which I had just bought brand new for a guinea; he gave me his instead. Several days later I visited him, and saw that he had had a silver case put over my box, on the cover of which was very elegantly engraved Apollo's harp and the following words: *Ex dono celeberrimi Josephi Haydn.* N.B. The Mis^tris gave me a stickpin as a souvenir.'   (CCLN 275)

Adulation without music did not suit Haydn, and one of the aspects of England he must have found most rewarding was the genuine interest in his music shown by the royal family. The Prince of Wales had been a frequent (if unpunctual) attender at Salomon's evenings, and he now busied himself promoting a private concert to be devoted to Haydn's music alone. It is some indication of the popularity Haydn enjoyed that even the king could be persuaded to attend – despite the presence of his son, and the absence of any music by Handel.

'On 1st February 1795, I was invited by the Prince of Wales

to attend a musical soirée at the Duke of York's, which the King, the Queen, her whole family, the Duke of Orange &c. attended. Nothing else except my own compositions was played; I sat at the pianoforte; finally I had to sing, too. The King, who hitherto could or would only hear Handel's music, was attentive; he chatted with me, and introduced me to the Queen, who said many complimentary things to me. I sang my German song, *"Ich bin der verliebteste".*'

(CCLN 305)

Haydn's honest account of his reception fails to mention various political incidents, however, which spoilt the first part of the entertainment; for these we have to turn to the oboist William Parke, who was one of the *virtuosi* present. In his entertaining *Musical Memoirs* he recalls:

'His Royal Highness the Duke of York gave a grand concert of instrumental music . . . at York House, Piccadilly, (where the Albany Chambers now stand,) at which their Majesties and the Princesses were present. Salomon led the band, amongst whom were Cervetto, the elder Parke, Shield, myself, Dance, Blake, and Haydn, who presided at the piano-forte. Jarnovicki was to have played a concerto on the violin, by desire of Her Majesty, who had never heard him perform; but on coming into the room just before the music commenced, and perceiving Salomon there, (to whom he bore a violent hatred,) Jarnovicki vented his spleen by leaving the house immediately. This insolent foreigner, who suffered professional jealousy to supersede the respect due to the queen of a great nation, deserved punishment for his presumption. When we had tuned our instruments, and were waiting for the signal to begin, His Royal Highness the Duke of Gloucester (brother to the King) entered the room, and fixing his eye on a respectable double-bass player, belonging to the Italian Opera, named *Jouve*, who had been several years in England, suddenly exclaimed, "There's a Frenchman!" and hurried out of the room. It ought not to appear extraordinary that persons of such exalted rank should have been mistrustful in times when the blind fury of the French Revolution had been so cruelly levelled at royalty, and when several instances had occurred of the British government finding it necessary to send Frenchmen out of the kingdom, one of whom, on taking leave of his friend, (an Italian musician,) said, "Fare ye well; I shall be back again in a fortnight with my friend *Buonaparte.*" Their Majesties, however, and the Princesses, sat in the room during the whole of the concert.

'At the end of the first part of the concert Haydn had the distinguished honour of being formally introduced to His Majesty George III, by His Royal Highness the Prince of Wales. My station at the time was so near to the King, that I could not avoid hearing the whole of their conversation. Amongst other observations, His Majesty said (in English) "Doctor Haydn, you have written a great deal." To which Haydn modestly replied, "Yes, Sire, a great deal more than is good." To which the King neatly rejoined, "Oh no, the world contradicts that."

'After his introduction, Haydn, by desire of the Queen, sat down to the piano-forte, and, surrounded by Her Majesty and her royal and accomplished daughters, sung, and accompanied himself admirably in several of his *canzonets.* The gracious reception Haydn experienced from the King was not only gratifying to *his* feelings, but flattering to the science he professed; and while it displayed the condescension and liberality of a great and good monarch, it could not fail proving a powerful stimulus to rising *genius.*

'The following week I attended a grand instrumental concert given by the Prince of Wales at Carlton House to their Majesties and the whole of the royal family. Haydn presided at the piano-forte, and Salomon led the band, which consisted of the same performers as at the Duke of York's. The magnificence of the scene on this occasion was truly fascinating. The exalted rank of those present, the splendour of the dresses, and the elegance and beauty of the ladies, all combined to strike the beholder with admiration and delight. I had permission that night to enter the room while the whole of the royal family (seventeen in number) were at supper. The King and Queen sat at the head of the table, and the branches of the royal family nearest to them,

CARLTON HOUSE, PALL MALL

according to their seniority, whilst the Prince of Wales occupied a seat opposite to his royal parents, doing the honours of his table with all that elegance for which he has ever been so highly distinguished. I frequently afterwards attended the concerts of the Prince of Wales, in one of which I played a concerted piece for the oboe, composed by Haydn, and was honoured with the distinguishing approbation of His Royal Highness, who, whilst playing the violoncello, called two foreign noblemen to him to listen, and repeatedly exclaimed "Bravi! – the finest tone in the world!" I had the satisfaction several times of meeting Haydn at Carlton House, at music parties, where, after the concert was ended, an elegant supper invited us to partake of its gratifications. The attentions we experienced at Carlton House proceeded from Mr Bect, then *maître d'hotel*, successor to Mr Weltjee, who had retired to his house and grounds at Chiswick Mall. Weltjee, who had been naturalised, kept a well-furnished table, which was frequented by several of the minor wits of the day; and he, being very proud of this little estate, felt great pleasure in showing his fields, his gardens, his hot-houses, &c., saying at the time, in his bad English, "Dish ish moine, dat ish moine; and, what ish more, I can leave it all to my posteriors" (posterity).' (Parke I 196–200)

Even Parke's garrulous account of events cannot entirely conceal the disturbing effect that revolutionary politics were having in England. Indeed, the whole series of royal performances may have been designed to compensate for the fact that Salomon's concerts had had to be suspended during the 1795 season, because of the impossibility of procuring 'Vocal Performers of the first talents' from abroad, owing to 'the present situation of affairs on the Continent'. Instead, Salomon had announced a co-operation with the Opera Concerts, under the leadership of the refugee Viotti,* 'who will also occasionally furnish new Pieces of Music'. Haydn's involvement in this 'Arrangement' guaranteed good houses, although the misfortunes of the year almost extended to a disaster in the very first concert.

'When Haydn appeared in the orchestra and seated himself at the Pianoforte, to conduct a symphony personally, the curious audience in the parterre left their seats and pressed forward towards the orchestra, with a view to seeing Haydn better at close range. The seats in the middle of the parterre were therefore empty, and no sooner were they empty but a great chandelier plunged down, smashed, and threw the numerous company into great confusion. As soon as the first moment of shock was over, and those who had pressed forward realized the danger which they had so luckily escaped, and could find words to express the same, many persons showed their state of mind by shouting loudly: "miracle! miracle!" Haydn himself was much moved, and thanked merciful Providence who had allowed it to happen that he could, to a certain extent, be the reason, or the machine, by which at least thirty persons' lives were saved. Only a few of the audience received minor bruises.

* Three years later, even Viotti was expelled from England under suspicion of being a Jacobin, despite protestations that he 'frequented no coffee-houses, belonged to no clubs, and had never in any situation uttered a word which could be deemed offensive to the British government' [Parke].

'This occurrence I have heard in various versions, almost always with the additional fact that the symphony has in London been given the complimentary name, "The Miracle". It may be that this is true, but when I asked Haydn about it, he said: "I know nothing of that." '

(Dies: Landon 287)

Sensationalism was not for Haydn. But the incident *did* actually occur, since it is mentioned (albeit casually) in the *Morning Chronicle* the following day ('. . . notwithstanding an interruption by the accidental fall of one of the chandeliers . . .'). The symphony in question, however, was No. 102, and not No. 96, which now carries the nickname.

The remainder of the concerts in the series (there were nine, rather than Salomon's normal twelve) went off without hitch. Dragonetti amazed by his agility on the double-bass, with a tone 'infinitely more pleasant than was ever before thought possible', and a Madame Gillberg from Sweden appeared as a wonder on the violin: 'she gave the *Double Stop* with considerable skill . . . Her person and manner are very interesting'. Evidently the war had not prevented all performers from seeking their fortunes in London.

Extra impetus was given to the musical season by the long-awaited marriage of the Prince of Wales to the Princess of Brunswick. In the celebratory flurry that followed, Haydn seems to have had to attend two different musical events on the same evening, to judge from his Notebooks:

'On the 10th, I was invited to a musical soirée at the Prince of Wales' in Carlton House. An old Symphony was played, which I accompanied on the pianoforte; then a Quartet; and afterwards I had to sing some German and English songs. The Princess sang with me, too; she played a Concerto on the pianoforte quite nicely.

'. . . On the 10th I was at the Covent Garden Theatre – to see the big Spectacul – *Windsor Castle, the music by Salomon quite passable*. The decorations – costumes – scenery, and the enormous amount of people on the stage are exaggerated. All the Gods of Heaven and Hell, and everything that lives on the earth are in the piece.' (CCLN 305–6, 299)

Haydn forgets to mention that he supplied an overture for this grand masque, which did indeed manage to include not only Peleus and Thetis, but also the Maid of Kent, the Black Prince and a harp concerto played by Mr Jones, the royal bard. Rather tactlessly, considering the occasion, the evening opened with a piece called *Life's Vagaries*, an infelicity which we hope the royal couple did not remark.

Haydn had now fulfilled his bargain with the Opera Concerts, and produced the last of his second set of symphonies, noting with relief on the first page 'The 12th which I have composed in England'. It is this work (No. 104) which carries the nickname of 'The London', and its first performance at his Benefit must have been one of the proudest moments of Haydn's life – as well as one of the most profitable. La Banti does not seem to have excelled in the cantata, *Scena di Berenice*, which he wrote specially for her, and his scathing parenthesis is in English, although the rest of the note is in German.

'On 4th May 1795, I gave my benefit concert in the Haymarket Theatre. The room was full of a select company. a) First part of the Military Symphony; Aria (Rovedino); Concerto (Ferlandy) for the first time; Duet (Morichelli and Morelli) by me; a new Symphony in D, the twelfth and last of the English; b) Second part of the Military Symphony; Aria (Morichelli); Concerto (Viotti); *Scena nuova* by me, Mad. Banti (She song very scanty). The whole company was thoroughly pleased and so was I. I made four thousand Gulden on this evening. Such a thing is only possible in England.' (CCLN 306)

The pressures on Haydn to remain in England must have seemed almost irresistible. He was richer than he had ever been before, with a total of twenty-four thousand gulden to his name, compared with the two thousand he had accumulated from his service with the Esterházys. He had the support of the English public, press and publishers: he had warm friends in all classes, and even a royal invitation to live at Windsor – the queen herself had offered him rooms there, adding slyly, 'and then sometimes we'll make music tête-à-tête'.

NEW ROOM, KING's THEATRE.

Dr. HAYDN's Night.

MONDAY, MAY 4, 1795.

PART I.

very good	Overture, MS. - - -	*Haydn.*
nothing fine	Song, Sig. ROVEDINO, - -	*Ferrari.*
Astonishing fine command of the Instrument, but degenerates into rather foolish trick	Concerto Hautbois, Sig. FERLENDIS, from Venice, (being his first Performance in this Country) -	*Ferlendis.*
very noisy	Duetto, Madame MORICHELLI and Sig. MORELLI, - -	*Haydn.*
	New Overture,	*Ditto.*

PART II.

Grand but very noisy	Military Symphony, - -	*Haydn.*
	Song, Madame MORICHELLI, -	*Paesiello.*
Most Delicious	Concerto Violin, Mr. VIOTTI,	*Viotti.*
Haydn sets a care-tive, but very little music in the composition	New Scene, Madame BANTI,	

DETAIL OF ANNOTATED PROGRAMME, 4 MAY 1795

'Oh! I'm not jealous of Haydn,' said the king, 'he's a good honest German man.' 'To keep that reputation', answered Haydn, 'is my greatest pride.'

Despite all offers and temptation, however, Haydn decided to return to Vienna. To the king he gave the excuses of loyalty to his former prince, plus a desire to see his fatherland and (more surprisingly) his wife again. When the king offered to have his wife sent over, Haydn hastily added that she would not even cross the Danube, let alone the Channel, and the threat was averted. In fact, there were many reasons that might have persuaded him to end his life in his native land. At sixty-three he deserved some sort of retirement, and the amount of effort that England had demanded from him would have been judged prodigious in a man half his age. At home was a court career, a reputation enhanced by his foreign successes and a steady pension from the Esterházys. Probably the threat of wartime privations also encouraged him to make the return journey now, while access to Europe was still open – although he had the tact not to mention this to the king. Many people were of the opinion that England's chances of victory were steadily diminishing, while the probability of her isolation was all too real. The shadow of Napoleon had fallen over London's music, and Haydn was too wise to ignore the warning signs.

So, while the Benefits continued and the season wound to an end, Haydn began to settle his accounts. One of the last advertised events to feature his music was indeed as curious as any connoisseur of English eccentricities could wish, a bizarre mixture of regal, educational, musical and social delights.

UNDER THE PATRONAGE OF
HIS ROYAL HIGHNESS THE PRINCE OF WALES
Order of the Evening Meeting for
READING AND MUSIC,
To be held at the NEW LYCEUM, HANOVER-SQUARE,
THIS PRESENT EVENING, JUNE 18,
in Honour of Their Royal Highness the PRINCE
and PRINCESS of WALES.

At Seven o'Clock – A LECTURE on ASTRONOMY,
illustrated by a large Transparent Diagram.
Eight o'Clock – ITALIAN, FRENCH, and ENGLISH READING.
Half past Eight – MUSIC, Vocal and Instrumental
Leader of the Band, Mr RAIMONDI.
Mr CLEMENTI will preside at the Piano Forte.
Overture – Dr HAYDN.
Song, Miss DUFOUR.
Concerto, Piano Forte. Miss MᶜARTHUR, CRAMER
Song, Signor TRISOBIO.
REFRESHMENTS
ITALIAN, FRENCH, and ENGLISH READINGS:
Sinfonia – HAYDN.
Concerto, Violin, Master PINTO SAUNDERS –
GIORNOVICHI.
Duet, Miss DUFOUR and Signor TRISOBIO.
FINALE.
(*True Briton* 18.vi.95)

We have no record of whether or not Haydn attended this
curious confection – he had obviously tired of noting every
royal event in his Notebook after the block entry: 'On 3rd
Feb. I was invited to the Prince of Wales'; on 15th, 17th and
19th Apr. 1795, I was there again, and on the 21st at the
Queen's in Buckingham House.'   (CCLN 305)
    Yet it is very probable that he did feel impelled to be there,
and also met Farington at the same entertainment, since a
complaint of his treatment by the royal family seems to have
slipped out, and found a place in Farington's *Diary* the
following day.

'Hadyn [*sic*], has attended the King & Queen, and at other
times the Prince of Wales, at least 40 times, and been kept
up, contrary to his usual hours, till one or two in a morning,
and yet never had the smallest pecuniary recompense from
any of them.'*   (Farington II 356)

---

* Eventually, in April the following year, Haydn had to write to the
Commissioners of Parliament to ask for the £100 which the Prince of
Wales owed him; he then received his money without delay.

Dealings with Salomon, on the other hand, were as punctilious as ever. Although there can hardly have been any need for a written agreement, Haydn added his signature to a document giving sole rights on the first six London symphonies to Salomon, and adding the opening bars of each work to preclude any possible confusion:

'The undersigned herewith testifies that, according to the agreement signed this day between myself and Herr Johan [*sic*] Peter Salomon, the afore-mentioned Herr Salomon shall have the exclusive rights pertaining to the following specified Overtures which I composed for his concerts; and that I hereby renounce any further claims whatever on him, now or at any other time. The afore-mentioned Overtures have the following *incipits*:

Executed at London this 13th of August 1795.
　　　　　Joseph Haydn [manu prop]ria.'　　(Landon 319)

Equally methodically, he drew up a list (in English) of all the works he had written in and for England between 1791 and 1795, adding the number of manuscript pages that each occupied; the total is an astounding 768 sheets, ranging from the symphonies and his (unperformed) opera to sets of minuets and German dances. Some of these works are now lost (the aria for the tenor Davide, for example, the setting of *God Save the King*, 'The Dream' – that is, the piece written to embarrass the German dilettante, the aria for Miss Poole and various dances). The remainder, however, represent a musical legacy to England which has never been repeated by any other visitor; nor has any other foreign musician declared as honestly as Haydn did to Griesinger that the days spent in England had been the happiest of his life. They had, he declared, 'opened a new world to him'.

Two days after signing the agreement with Salomon, Haydn left England. Amongst his souvenirs was a present from Clementi, a cup made out of a coconut and tastefully decorated with silver; a silver shield, presented to him by W. D. Tattersall for the settings he had contributed to the *Improved Psalmody*; the libretto for a possible oratorio to be called *The Creation*; and a talking parrot.

He also left with plans for providing 'new and original music' for English publishers over the next five years, providing only that he 'shall so long live and continue in health so as to be capable of writing and composing musick'. Although he failed to fulfil many of these commitments (symphonies are mentioned, for instance), it is touching to see that the contract, drawn up by Hyde the following year to

DETAIL OF THE HAYDN–HYDE CONTRACT

send to Vienna, was witnessed by Rebecca Schroeter;
despite the apparent silence, her interest in Haydn's well-
being was undiminished.

'As *good* a creature as *great Musician*' was Burney's verdict;
and when the little libretto that Haydn took away with him
had flowered several years later, the energetic Doctor was
tireless in raising subscribers for the publication. All
Haydn's English friends are listed, from 'His Majesty *The
King of Great Briton*' and all the royal family (two copies) to
'The Revd Thomas Twining, M:^{ris} Schroeter, and Mr.
J:P:Salomon' (with twelve copies). Burney could well con-
gratulate himself: 'I procured him more subscribers to that
sublime effort of Genius – the Creation, than all his other
friends, whether at home or abroad, put together.' The
English never forgot Haydn.

A FOOTNOTE

It would be unkind to omit from the roll-call of English enthusiasts our friend William Gardiner, who never forgot the composer he had spied in 1791. In 1804, he sent the following letter via Salomon:

'To Joseph Haydn, Esq., Vienna.

Sir, – For the many hours of delight which your musical compositions have afforded me, I am emboldened (although a stranger) to beg your acceptance of the enclosed small present, wrought in my manufactory at Leicester. It is no more than six pairs of cotton stockings, in which is worked that immortal air "God preserve the Emperor Francis," with a few other quotations from your great and original productions. Let not the sense I have of your genius be measured by the insignificance of the gift; but please to consider it as a mark of the great esteem I bear to him who has imparted so much pleasure and delight to the musical world.

I am, dear Sir, with profound respect, your most humble servant,

William Gardiner'
(Gardiner *Music and Friends* 362–3)

He later noted that 'the subjects quoted, and wrought on the fabric of the stockings, were the following: – "My mother bids me bind my hair" [*English Canzonetta*]; the bass solo of "The Leviathan" [*The Creation*]; the andante in the surprise sinfonia; his sonata "*Consummatum est*" [*Seven Last Words*]; and "God preserve the Emperor."' However, 'the war was raging at the time, and as Mr Salomon had no reply, we concluded it never arrived at its place of destination . . .'

BIBLIOGRAPHY

REFERENCES TO SOURCES

Angelo	Angelo, Henry: *Reminiscences*. London 1830.
Arblay	d'Arblay, Frances (=Fanny Burney): *Memoirs of Dr Burney*. London 1832.
Bombet: Gardiner	Bombet, L. A. C.: *The Life of Haydn* (trans: William Gardiner). London 1817.
Burney	Burney, Charles: *A General History of Music*. London 1782–9.
CCLN	Landon, H. C. R.: *The Collected Correspondence and London Notebooks of Joseph Haydn*. London 1959.
Dies: Landon	Dies, A. C.: *Biographische Nachrichten von Joseph Haydn* (trans: Landon). Vienna 1810.
Farington	ed. Garlick, K. and Macintyre, A.: *The Diary of Joseph Farington*, Vols I & II. New Haven and London 1978.
Gardiner	Gardiner, William: *Sights in Italy with Some Account of the Present State of Music and the Sister Arts in that Country*. London 1847.
Holcroft	*Memoirs of the late Thomas Holcroft*. London 1816.
Jackson	Jackson, William: *Observations on the Present State of Music in London*. 2nd edition, London 1791.
Landon	Landon, H. C. R.: *Haydn: Chronicle and Works. Haydn in England 1791–1795*. London 1976.
Lonsdale	Lonsdale, R.: *Dr Charles Burney*. Oxford 1965.

115

Moritz	Moritz, Charles: *Travels chiefly on foot through several parts of England in 1782*. London 1795.
Papendiek	Papendiek, Charlotte: *Court and Private Life in the Time of Queen Charlotte*. London 1887.
Parke	Parke, W. T.: *Musical Memoirs*, 2 vols. London 1830.
Rees	Rees, Abraham: *The Cyclopaedia: or Universal Dictionary of Arts, Sciences and Literature*. London 1819.
Twining	Twining, Thomas: *Recreations and Studies of a Country Clergyman of the Eighteenth Century*. London 1882.
Wendeborn	Wendeborn, G. F. A.: *A View of England towards the close of the 18th Century*. London 1791.
Wesley	Wesley, Samuel: *Reminiscences* (1836 et seq). British Library Add MS 27513.
Wesley	Wesley: *Lectures*. British Library Add MS 35015.

ADDITIONAL SOURCES

Gardiner, William:	*Music and Friends*. London 1838.
Gotwals, V.:	Haydn: *Two Contemporary Portraits*. Madison, Milwaukee and London 1968.
Griesinger, G. A.:	*Biographische Notizen über Joseph Haydn*. Leipzig 1810.